Freshwater Fishing

Keith A. Rogers

Leisure Press
Champaign, Illinois

Developmental Editor: Sue Ingels Mauck
Copy Editor: Claire M. Mount
Assistant Editor: Janet Beals
Production Director: Ernie Noa
Typesetter: Sandra Meier
Text Design: Keith Blomberg
Text Layout: Denise Mueller
Cover Design: Conundrum Designs
Cover Photo: Mark Kelley/Alaska Photo
Illustrations By: Douglas E. Klapperich
Printed By: Versa Press

ISBN: 0-88011-185-2

Library of Congress Cataloging-in-Publication Data

Rogers, Keith A.
  Freshwater fishing.

  Summary: An experienced fisherman discusses the
knowledge, attitudes, and techniques necessary for
pleasurable and successful fishing.
  1. Fishing. [1. Fishing. 2. Fishes] I. Title.
SH441.R66 1987   799.1   84-10013
ISBN 0-88011-185-2

Printed in the United States of America

10 9 8 7 6 5 4 3 2 1

Leisure Press
A division of Human Kinetics Publishers, Inc.
Box 5076, Champaign, IL 61820
1-800-DIAL-HKP
1-800-334-3665 (in Illinois)

35953

To Howard and Gert,
who have practiced patience since day one.

Acknowledgments

My special thanks goes to Marian Green, a friend, angler, and journalist who edited the initial manuscript and who shared with me her appreciation for the great outdoors.

And to my fishing buddies Frank Albert, Ron Sittinger, Fen Truebridge, Rick Bruegel, Steve Yungner, Joe Voelker, Sam LaBella, Mel Nelson, Eric Lawrence, Ron Weiand, Mike Zampa, Jack Berman, Bruce Bartholomew, Katy Green, Gary Rogers, and Mike Sapunor whom I relied on heavily for anecdotes and techniques. To Thierry Robin, a friend from France who survived Honker Bay; and Tom and Beverly Laine, the "bait man" and "bait lady," who offered us dry clothes, their warm friendship, and sound advice. To Fred Brown and Jeff Williams and the guys at Harris Harbor who found my boat and to Giz Galli who brought us back.

My thanks goes to Alex Mihalka, Joe Hanus, Mark Penner, Rick Hanson, Bill Templeton, Stan Kossen, and the Danville, California Tigers portable computer club for their technical assistance. And to Sue Ingels Mauck for her cooperation and ideas on structuring the manuscript.

I am especially indebted to photographers Michael Macor, Kurt Rogers, Thomas Ovalle, and Randy Becker who worked odd hours to capture on film the essence of fishing. And to John D. O'Connor, a colleague who always said that I should write a book about fishing.

This book would not have been possible without the artistry of Paul B. Johnson, whose illustrations of freshwater game fish species were used by permission of Dave Dick of the California Department of Fish and Game. Nor would the species illustrations have been complete without the cooperation of John Klingbil of Wisconsin's fisheries management department.

A special thanks goes to Douglas E. Klapperich for illustrating the mechanics of knot tying and fly rodding. And to Tony Alvarez of the

Livermore, California fly fishing club who demonstrated the basic techniques of fly casting.

And, I owe thanks to Darrell Lowrance and Thayne Smith of Lowrance Electronics, Inc. in Tulsa, Oklahoma, who, through the vast resources of their company, continue to preserve and promote U.S. sport fisheries, and who allowed me to use illustrations and technical information from their *New Guide to the Fun of Electronic Fishing*.

World records and factual information about fish habits and history were based on records kept by the International Game Fish Association in Fort Lauderdale, Florida, a valuable resource for all anglers.

I also appreciate the cooperation of Ed Rice and Robert Brown of the International Sportmen's Expositions, who allowed me to use their photograph of Les Anderson's world-record king salmon.

And finally to all the anglers who back organizations like John Beuttler's United Anglers of California and Barry Canevaro's California Striped Bass Association.

Contents

Preface

When I first got into it, fishing was a sport that I did with my dad on his days off during the summer in Indiana. We fished primarily for large-mouth bass but devoted a good fraction of our efforts to catching catfish, crappie, and bluegill.

Fishing is something I now do year-round in California whenever I get the time. Primarily, I go after anadromous fish: trophy-size, migratory fish like salmon and striped bass which spawn in freshwater rivers but grow up in the briny blue of the Pacific Ocean.

Whether it's in Indiana or California, the fundamentals of the sport are still the same. I wrote this book as a general guide to freshwater game fishing. It explains techniques for the novice angler and spans the spectrum of the sport. As is often the case in sports, what the sportsman knows is based on experience. I keep records of when and where I caught fish and how I caught them. I rely on this history to plan future trips and make subtle adjustments in techniques that I believe will produce results.

Much of the success in fishing, perhaps a large percentage of it, relies on understanding the role that fish play in nature's scheme. To catch fish is to know what they're eating. Then, it's a matter of fashioning an object that resembles this and presenting it to them in such a manner that they'll accept it.

To do this, one must understand the nature of a fish's environment including water temperature, clarity, current, depth, and subsurface geological structure. It's often a nuts-and-bolts, commonsense type of challenge. Today's technology with paper graph and liquid crystal display electronic depth-finding equipment has eliminated some of the question marks. There are still many that remain.

Different fish prefer different appetizers; some don't want to eat anything. It's important, therefore, to show them something that will make them mad enough to strike. Under some conditions, weather and otherwise, fish won't bite no matter what adjustments are made.

The differences in fish, both biologically and in their responses to artificial bait, are explained according to species. This book includes a field guide to freshwater species, with world records kept by the International Game Fish Association.

I attempt to explain the importance of preserving the sport through sound ecological practices and fisheries management. The future of sportfishing depends not only on the abilities of state and federal governments to protect it but also on the individual angler to preserve it.

In the 30 years that I've been fishing, from Virginia to California and from Arkansas to Alaska, I've learned that some aspects of it never change. It always takes a lot of patience and some degree of luck. A skilled angler is one who has learned from mistakes. This book is a collection of my learning experiences.

Keith Rogers
Berkeley, California

Introduction

It is breezy this morning on San Francisco Bay. With each gust that whips through the harbor, the halyards on the masts of more than a hundred sailboats clang in unison. It is an eerie sound. But it is the sound of the harbor, a safe place, perhaps the only place to be in a boat when the weather is bad.

Despite age or experience, anglers will sometimes do anything to go fishing. They'll take tiny aluminum boats and embark on high seas with rolling waves and shifting tides, hoping that on the other side they'll find a sheltered cove.

They are no different from those who stalk wide, roily rivers in chest waders searching for a place shallow enough to cross. They wade out about halfway and then realize that it's going to be tough to reach either shore.

During the course of writing this book, I encountered a wide range of weather conditions. At times it was calm enough to put a rod out the back of my 25-foot cabin cruiser while I plucked out a chapter on a portable word processor. There were other times, though, when the wind blew rollers into the brunt of a tide being pushed by the downstream force of the Sacramento and San Joaquin rivers.

A 25-foot boat is generally big enough to handle most adverse weather conditions. But the forces of nature can dwarf a vessel that size and bigger. I've seen the Pacific Ocean toss around a 13-foot-thick trunk of a redwood tree like it was a small toothpick caught in a giant whirlpool.

Because fishing is a water sport, always give an extra thought to safety. Think before you fish. Always have a backup system: Carry extra spark plugs for your outboard motor and a patch-kit for your chest waders. Don't wear a pair of boots that you can't kick off if you happen to fall overboard. If you're out on a lake and a storm comes up, get to the nearest shore. Know your boat's capabilities and learn how to use them. Don't get stuck halfway across the river.

No one will scoff at you if you let a few of the big ones get away, as long as you live to tell about it. Fish know how to swim, so should you.

chapter 1

Patience

Buck called it the world's worst backlash. Being the father of two young boys, he had seen his share of what some fishermen call monofilament bird nests, the kind that happen when a fledgling angler forgets to use his thumb to slow the spool of a bait-casting reel during an attempt to hurl a lure to the far side of a lake.

"This is disgusting," Buck said, sweat dripping from his brow as he sat in Indiana's 90° humidity trying to unravel the mess of line.

He tussled with it for a few minutes. Then, like magic, he pulled the right pigtail protruding from the mess and the spool of my level-wind reel spun free. He then cranked up the slack, splashed the moss off of the lure, and demonstrated the proper casting technique.

As soon as the spinner hit the surface, he cranked the reel in a steady rhythm, making the spinner crawl down the roots of the stump until it was swimming in the direction of the boat.

"Now that's how it's done," Buck said.

He made a second cast to the other side of the stump which sent out a ring of ripples across the mirror-like surface of Cataract Lake. This time he cranked the spinner more slowly as if he were waiting for a bass to catch up with it. Seeing that this was not the case, he reeled rapidly so that the twin blades on the spinner fluttered as it rose to the surface.

This time he punched the release button on his reel and held the spool in place with his thumb. Then with his left hand, he reached for the toothpick that was always wedged in the corner of his mouth when he fished and twirled it once.

"This is my last cast, then you can try it." I never forgot those words.

He paused for a moment to watch a flock of ducks fly across the horizon until their hook-shaped formation vanished behind a stand of maples. He always watched birds when we fished and would often say "That's a diver" or "That's a puddler." The divers were almost always fish-eating ducks like merganzers or grebes. Fish ducks did not taste as good in the skillet as puddlers. But the fish ducks meant fish were close by, and Buck was about to prove it.

He announced that a bass was hiding in the shadow of that stump. The next thing I heard was my fiberglass rod whisking past my ear as he sidearmed a cast that sunk the lure into a shady patch of water about two feet from the jagged side of the stump. His thumb slowed the spool so that it didn't unravel out of control.

This time he turned the crank handle immediately, causing the spinner's blades to purr as the lure disappeared into the shadow. Buck slowed his retrieve a bit, and this time the water welled up by the stump. The rod suddenly bounced with life.

"Get the net ready," he hollered to my older brother, Gary, who was sitting in the bow of the boat.

Buck bit down on his toothpick, exposing his front teeth while he fought the fish. With his index finger, he adjusted the star drag on the side of his reel just enough to match the line tension to the weight of the fish.

He did not yank back while the fish shook its head. Instead, he kept the rod tip high, driving the barb of the hook into the bass's lip, sinking it deeper into the tough part of its flesh as he applied gradual pressure.

Water sprayed when the bass's dark, bronze body shot to the surface as it tried to evade its captors in the boat. Line slicked off of Buck's reel each time the fish lunged for the deep. After three lunges, Buck worked the fish toward the boat. Its football-sized body flashed below.

The bass was intent on fighting its last seconds near the back of the boat where it threatened to wrap the 8-pound monofilament test line around the propeller. I grabbed the net from my brother, but even while leaning over the side I was still not in position to land the largemouth.

Buck grabbed the net from me. He held it with his right hand and with the rod in his left, he raised the rod tip high so that the bass nosed toward the surface.

When it was clear of the outboard motor, Buck slid the big green net under it and hoisted the squirming fish into the boat. It slapped its tail violently on the floor of the boat, showing that it was more disgusted with being caught than Buck was with my backlash.

He slipped his thumb into the mouth of the bass and then pinched its lower lip with his forefinger. That was enough to paralyze it briefly so he could slide it into a chainlink basket that he'd snap to an oarlock and hang over the side. The basket was actually a wire mesh contraption with a spring-loaded trap door. It kept fish alive in case we wanted to release some later.

I learned at an early age that it takes patience to learn how to cast. And, it takes patience to tie knots and bait hooks and unravel backlashes. It even takes patience to wait for Dad to finish demonstrating the proper casting technique.

Fundamentals

There's a lot more to the fundamentals of fishing than using sharp hooks and keeping the rod tip high when fighting a fish. Although these are two essential aspects of the sport, every angler must also have some basic knowledge of the type of fish that he or she is trying to catch and how that particular species fits in with the food chain and the habitat of the lake, pond, river, stream, or bay.

Once a decision has been made to go after a certain type of fish in a specific environment, the angler must then select the proper equipment. This equipment should be designed to get the job done, yet conform to the angler's ability whether he or she is casting from the shore of a lake, wading a river, or drifting in a boat.

   The angler must then decide whether to use bait or artificial lures, flies, spoons, spinners or jigs. Then it's a matter of presenting one of these things to the fish so they'll instinctively strike it because of hunger, aggravation, or from behavior spurred by spawning and territorial instincts. The art of presentation involves many factors including color, size, and action. Adjustments must be made for water clarity, current, and depth. Many of the less understood behavioral patterns of fish are also affected by the cloudiness of the sky, the position of the sun and moon, and the barometric pressure.

The Scope
of Freshwater Fishing

Factors that influence freshwater fish will be discussed in detail later as will tips on how to play and land fish. But first, to get a better understanding of what freshwater fishing entails, consider the example of how to entice catfish, which are found throughout the continental United States.

   It doesn't take much thought to figure out why catfish go on the rampage every August in Indiana, just after the big females or "hen" fish have come off the nest. It happens about the same time catalpa trees become infested with a caterpillar-like insect, a bug the Hoosiers call the catalpa worm. I spent hours when I was 13 climbing those broad-leafed lady cigar trees to pluck bucketfuls of the black-and-yellow parasites that were making tobacco out of God's greenery.

   Catalpa worms, I discovered, were very effective for enticing channel catfish and flathead catfish which swam the rivers and lakes where catalpa trees dotted the shoreline.

   It was perfect natural bait in those parts, especially in August when an occasional breeze would knock a few strays into the water for the "whiskerjaws" to sniff. Had the water in those muddy rivers been more clear, it would have been possible to devise a wooly worm-type fly patterned after a catalpa worm that might have worked for catfish. But the design of the fish itself, custom-made for hunting food by sense of smell and feeding primarily off of the bottom, made it an easier fish to entice with something that was smelly and juicy rather than something that only looked attractive; although occasionally one could be fooled by a spinner or lure that had the flash and action of a minnow.

There was a trick to using catalpa worms that I learned from an old-timer at a bait shop. He would hoard catalpa worms which he gathered in the summer and freeze them so that when spring came he would have plenty on hand for the months when catalpa worms weren't to be found.

Channel catfish are often called "fiddlers" because of the finicky manner in which they bite. They'll pick up the scent of bait and investigate it with long whiskers which protrude from the corners of their mouths. Instead of swallowing their dinner in one big bite, they chomp at it one piece at a time, giving the angler the impression that they're fiddling around with it.

There's something about the skin of a catalpa worm that makes it stick to a hook when it's soaked in water for a few seconds. The guts of the worm, hanging inside out, enhance the scent it puts in the water and is twice as effective for attracting fish. And, once a fiddler finds the bait, it has to do more than just fiddle around to get that sticky skin off of the hook. Naturally, this helps the angler set the hook. So the technique for catching catfish in Indiana waterways where catalpa trees lined the banks was to thread catalpa worms on a hook inside out so that their skins stuck to the hooks and their guts put out a scent that was naturally appetizing to the predatory catfish.

Characteristics of Fish

A fish is a cold-blooded animal, a predator of its own kind that is territorial and sensitive to changes in temperature, pressure, and aquatic conditions. Fish react to color, scent, and movement. They strike when a bait is presented to them properly and when it is conducive to their seasonal habits. Fish that are about ready to spawn seem to be more aggressive, perhaps because they simply need more food to compensate for a rapid gain in body weight.

Being quiet is almost as great a virtue as being patient when it comes to fishing. Fish are more sensitive to noise than many human beings. They don't have floppy ears, but many species of fish have skin so sensitive to vibrations that they can sense a human voice at the surface.

Fish have evolved in accordance to their habitat. Their bodies are custom-made for their living conditions. Some have large nostrils and feelers or *barbels* that probe through murky water in search of food. Others have large eyes that provide wide peripheral vision. It is important to remember that fish live in a suspended environment. They have both vertical and lateral movement capabilities and their vision allows them in most cases to simultaneously span an area above, below, and to the sides.

Fish rely on gills instead of lungs for breathing. Some fish have scales, others have skin. Some have teeth, others have large mouths. A typical freshwater fish has a lateral line that runs from the fork of its tail to its gill plate. The lateral line is an organ that is sensitive to vibrations. It is a line of pores that can sense current and pressure from other fish nearby. Trout can hear a human tiptoeing because of the sensitivity of their nerve-muscles. And, depending on the water conditions, they can see a shadow stalking about the water's surface near their hideouts.

Striped bass, which range from coast to coast in the United States and have been transplanted in hundreds of freshwater lakes, are equally sensitive to vibrations, daylight conditions, and odors. Like their cousins the white and yellow bass, striped bass were created with lines on their sides that correspond to an underlying red-colored muscle area. This muscle helps the fish feed at night by detecting vibrations sent out by smaller baitfish fluttering to escape their predators.

Fish have a unique way of suspending their bodies in water, and a way of effortlessly propelling themselves through water because of air bladders and, especially, fins that protrude from their bodies. Usually two pelvic fins help a fish swim, and a dorsal fin or pair of dorsal fins on its back allows it to change directions and defend itself against predators.

I used to wear rubber-soled boots or tennis shoes to stalk the banks of Lake Del Valle in northern California to keep from scaring the stripers away before I tossed plugs at them. The plugs had beads inside that would rattle and agitate the water, sending out vibrations to arouse the striking instincts of nearby fish. Some lures designed for large game fish have flimsy rubber tails that flop back and forth in the water. This action produces the same type of vibrations that the baitfish, the food of these predators, produce.

Outfitting

Fishing is a sport of preparation. A wise fisherman always checks the weather conditions before he sets out. There's nothing more disgusting than a fishing partner who has to come in early because he forgot the temperature on the lake was 10° colder than when he left home. Some anglers might have been better off swimming after the critters by the time they got soaked to the bone in a rainstorm waiting for their bobbers to go under. The same holds true for the fair-haired mosquito swatter who forgot what color skin gets before it blisters. There is no place in the outdoors for one who complains. In the years that I've fished rivers, lakes, streams, and bays, no one has ever caught a fish by complaining. But many were caught by those who were prepared not only for the fish but also for the weather and all the other elements of the great outdoors.

Experienced stream anglers have their boots soled with indoor-outdoor carpeting to give them better footing on moss-covered rocks. They take with them a wading staff when encountering stiff currents. A staff can be quickly fashioned from a hickory branch.

Don't try to walk against a stiff current when exiting a stream. Walk slightly downstream for lesser resistance from the current but make sure to probe ahead to avoid stepping in deep holes.

When casting from lake shorelines, wear tennis shoes for sure, quiet footing and for plowing through Southern bogs. Always wear tennis shoes, deck shoes, or slipover boots when out on a boat. The key here is to have footwear that can easily be kicked off in case you fall overboard.

Anyone who is shoreline fishing in the arid West where rattlesnakes are found should wear hard-soled, high-topped, leather walking boots and carry a snakebite kit, just in case a rattler strikes.

Three Cardinal Rules

Anglers should abide by three cardinal rules. Be a sport, be safe, and keep the environment clean.

All fish that are caught for the sport of it should be handled in such a manner that they can be released unharmed. The ultimate sport angler is the person who fishes with a fly rod, uses barbless hooks, and releases everything he or she catches. If you plan to catch a fish for dinner, you should at least abide by the limit laws and never keep an under-sized fish.

The rules, which all states have, ensure plentiful fish populations so that everyone may have an opportunity to catch fish.

Be safe when fishing. I've fished places where it was so crowded,

I contemplated wearing a hard hat and elbow pads to protect myself from errant casts. Hooks in ears are no fun. Always consider safety factors pertaining to weather and water conditions.

Don't leave your trash behind. Many of us go fishing simply to enjoy the great outdoors. Not only is littering against the law, such things as tangled lines and discarded lure wrappers can damage an outboard motor should it plow through that garbage. More than one foot has been cut by a dropped bottle that shattered on the river rocks. Take all trash with you.

Figure 2.1. (opposite page) California angler Joe Voelker stalks Hot Creek in the Sierra Nevada range for native rainbow trout. Bends and undercut banks of mountain streams are good places in which to find trout. Photo: Keith Rogers

chapter 2

How to
locate fish

A Caspian tern cupped its wings and glided into a gray sky, hovering over the cove at Del Valle dam. The lake shimmered below in the predawn light like a sheet of tin foil rippling in a gentle breeze.

The graceful, white bird kept its head cocked as it soared, hoping to spot the silhouette of a striped bass which was herding a school of threadfin shad to the surface.

The tern let out a shrill cry when it spotted the bass. It immediately tucked its wings and plummeted to the surface where threadfins were squirming in all directions. The silvery shad must have looked like sparklers going off to the wary bird as it hit the water with a splash and brought its buoyant frame to a halt. Instantly, with outstretched wings, the bird powered itself back to flight carrying with it the cargo of an injured shad whose fate would have been the same had the bass caught up with it.

Frank Albert noticed this activity from behind a poplar tree growing at the edge of the boulder-cragged dam. He watched as the bird landed on a buoy across the cove to digest its breakfast. Then he reached into his coat pocket and grabbed a long box containing a blue-and-silver colored plug that was shaped like a minnow but jointed at its tail. It had three treble hooks and a short plastic lip that caused it to dig through the water less than six inches beneath the surface.

Quickly, he tied the plug to the end of his line, grabbed his spinning rod, and stepped lightly over the rocks. He went unnoticed by all the wildlife, until he stood directly in front of the place where the tern had spotted the bass. With his boots spread shoulder-length apart, he maintained his balance on a large, flat boulder so it would not tip back and forth and send vibrations into the stillness of the lake.

Frank hurled the lure to the left of where the bass had slaughtered the shad. It landed with a plunk and immediately vanished below the surface when he turned the reel's handle. He made dozens of casts to that area, working a pie-shaped sector from his left to his right. Each time, he reeled the instant the plug hit the water. Once in a while he fluctuated the speed of his retrieve, causing the lure to dart like a scared shad.

Two more birds circled the cove, focusing their beady eyes on the water below. They let out several shrieks and began diving near the center of the cove beyond Frank's casting range. Each time they swooped they edged closer to Frank's rock. He lofted a cast which carried with the wind and landed at the position of high noon on the imaginary clock-face before him. He cranked the handle erratically, slowing a bit as the plug moved into shallower water. The birds were frightened by his next cast, which landed at the two o'clock position.

This time he made the plug swim along at a fast clip angled toward the rock pile. When it reached the shallow shelf running parallel to the shoreline, the water churned. A large tail fin appeared and slammed the water three times. Frank's rod froze taut and pointed to where the bass had surfaced. He shouted, ''Fish on.'' His reel screamed but then stopped suddenly.

He ripped his lure in when it floated to the surface. Everything was in good condition except for some paint chipped near the front hook. That hook was entangled with the center hook, which explained why the bass got away. He continued to cast the rest of the morning but never got a strike. Even the birds flew away.

The day had not been fruitless. Though he was restricted to the shoreline, he had managed to locate fish in a lake without relying on electronic gadgetry. The birds' keen eyesight located the fish for him. More important, though, was understanding why fish were there at that time of day.

Hangouts and Hiding Places

The boulders of Del Valle Dam provided an excellent place for baitfish to live where they could easily hide in the crevices formed by piles of underwater rocks. Largemouth bass and striped bass also found the Del Valle Dam to be a good location to stalk their prey in the dim, early morning light. The stairstep-style rock shelf dropping from 10 to 35 feet and then falling off into a 90-foot hole gave the bass an ideal place to patrol the open water areas of the cove until they could drive the baitfish into the shallow shelf and slay them before they had a chance to duck into the rocks.

The conditions were right for an early morning feed from the predatory fish. It was winter, and the larger females were fattening up with eggs that they would drop in the spring. Any small fish they could chase down, a shad, small trout, squawfish, or juvenile largemouth bass, fueled their appetites.

The wind direction was also in Frank's favor. It had been blowing from the east every afternoon for the past three days. This meant that plankton, the microscopic plant and animal life that smaller fish thrive on, had been blown like paper dots into the cove formed by the dam.

He noticed the surface activity, so he tossed a plug designed to run just under the lake's surface. Its jointed body sent vibrations through the surface. Vibrations travel faster through water than through air. A line of scales stretching from nose to tail on both sides of a bass receives sonar vibrations and delivers them through nerve endings to the fish's inner ear. Bass don't have ear portals like humans and other animals. Their whole body acts as an ear which hears its prey moving through the water.

Frank went to one spot to cast. He did not try other locations along the bank. His philosophy was to go to the place where he had seen fish before and work that area thoroughly, hoping fish would come within casting distance.

There's an old saying that's been handed down through generations of anglers. Either you can go out looking for fish or you can wait for them to come to you. Both ways produce results depending on the fishing conditions and the type of fish. Location, species, and time of year make a difference.

A person fishing with bait will have better luck going to one place on a lake or river where fish are likely to frequent and waiting for them to come by. A plug caster should work an area out thoroughly and then move to the next likely spot if nothing happens. Once you find where they are, keep fishing it until you turn the strikes into catches. Remember the area through landmarks and water conditions and begin fishing there on the next outing.

How long should you wait at a certain hole for fish to bite? That depends on the reputation of the place. If it has produced fish in the past, give it more time than a place that is unproven. I like to go where I've found fish before and wait for them to show up.

The best example I can recall is my experience with fishing the China Cove basin of Honker Bay near the mouth of the Sacramento River in California. I always waited longer for striped bass to show up in China Cove but once they did, my catch was usually bigger, pound-for-pound, than in other places I had tried. I used a natural bait, in this case a catfish-like staghorn sculpin, about six inches long. The result: a 68-pound limit of striped bass, two 20-pounders and one 28-pound linesider. They all hit within a two-hour period and all fell for the same bait: a sculpin which had been creased at its forehead by a well-honed fillet knife.

Keeping Records

Two months later I returned to the same location with only a mudsucker, about the size of a pinky finger. Using light monofilament line, I snelled a special one-ought hook to match the size of the mudsucker and cast it at the brink of an outgoing tide. That was enough to convince a 43-pound striper to mouth the bait and fight viciously for the next 45 minutes.

Now, every time I go fishing I jot down in a log book where I fished, what I fished with, what the conditions were, and what I caught, even if it was nothing. I use this information to plan future outings and locate fish when the conditions, such as the season, the time of day or night, moon phases, and tidal flows, are similar.

Time of Day and Season

Many factors affect the location of game fish at a given time of day. I've found large lake bass feeding wildly 25 feet beneath the surface on the eve of a spring rainstorm. As the water warms approaching summer they move into shallower water to spawn and find food.

Lunkers move into the shallows in the evenings and mornings to feed on smaller fish. In bays and rivers where tides have a more drastic effect on water levels, shallow sandbars make good choices for locating fish on the incoming tide. You should move to the deep sides of these bars on the outgoing tide to catch the reverse effect. As water moves off a shallow, flat area it washes food and baitfish into the deeper channels.

Land Formations

I've always had good luck fishing a point of land from either boat or shore. Points of land or other natural geologic formations such as cliffs, larger rock shelves, and shallow gravel bars jutting from a river bank form natural holding areas for plankton and baitfish.

To locate fish, you must think like them. Put yourself in their fins and swim around for a while. If you were a muskellunge or a northern pike, for example, you might be found hiding in a weed bed at the bottom of a deep hole during the daylight hours. Another good spot for a pike to launch an attack on a school of nonobservant perch is in the shade of a log or overhanging bank.

Fish go where their appetites take them. Locating fish often involves identifying a particular structure or geologic feature. Underwater ledges are natural hangouts for schooling fish. Predators, such as largemouth bass, walleye, and pike, seek shade to conceal their identity while waiting for traveling baitfish. The shade of logs, trees, or rock formations are good places to locate these game fish.

Rainbow trout hide along undercut banks in stream bends or behind a boulder in a stiff, moving current. Feeder streams which dump into larger streams or rivers are natural trout hangouts. To see trout before they see you, use a pair of polarized sunglasses to eliminate glare from sparkling streams and rivers. Be sure to sneak up on them, crawling on your hands and knees if necessary. Even with these precautionary efforts, more often than not they'll see you before you see them.

Ripples and Waterfalls

Waterfalls are beautiful, especially to the angler who is looking for fish. Common sense will explain why bass and other predatory fish search for food at the base of waterfalls. It's no different from cows turned loose in a bare field next to a grain elevator. When the chute starts kicking out corn, the cows come around. The same is true for fish at a waterfall, drainage pipe, or anyplace where fast moving water dumps food into a stream.

To find fish near a waterfall, cast a heavy, shiny spoon or a 1/2- to 1-ounce lead-headed jig parallel to the edge of the whitewater. You need something heavy to get down in the current where fish are holding. Deep-diving action lures and heavy spinners will work, but spoons and jigs are sometimes more productive around waterfalls where food flashes by.

On their way upstream to spawn, king salmon will hold in the deep holes of rivers in the Pacific Northwest. In years when river levels are low, or when fall rains come later than normal, salmon will remain in the holes until rainfall increases the river's flow to the point where they can go "hole hopping" upriver until they reach the very stream where they were hatched.

The secret in locating salmon is to find the river's deepest parts, those capable of holding hundreds of fish, then rig your equipment so that your bug or bait will be presented near the bottom. Whether it's a fly or a spoon, roe or anchovy, you've got to get it near the bottom.

A fly caster will generally need a high-density or super high-density shooting head, maybe even lead core line to present his or her fly at

Figure 2.2. A fly caster and a boatload of bait anglers in a drift boat fish the same hole for salmon on Oregon's Chetco River.   Photo: Keith Rogers

the bottom of swift, deep holes. Likewise, a spincaster either tossing a spoon or drifting roe will need an assortment of split shot to give his or her line the proper drift.

Wind Patterns

Wind patterns are equally important to the angler looking for concentrations of plankton. With electronic fish-locating equipment, these microorganisms show up as masses of tiny dots on graph paper. Because plankton are so light-weight, they tend to be carried with water currents or wind that blows across the surface of a lake or bay. For example, if the wind has been blowing from the west to the east over a duration of days, plankton will tend to concentrate near the east shores of that particular lake, having been rushed there by the wind. Professional black bass anglers will go to a spot where they have detected plankton and begin casting on the premise that a game fish will investigate whatever smaller variety of fish is attracted to the plankton.

Contour Maps

Structures such as submerged trees, logs, or brushpiles hold large amounts of plankton. This fact alone makes these structures ideal habitats for schools of black and white crappie.

One way to locate these structures in a reservoir without having to rely on electronic depth sounders is to go to a public library or write the United States Geological Survey (USGS) for contour maps illustrating the watershed before it was dammed. The USGS also has inland river and lake maps; the U.S. Coast Guard can supply navigational charts for most bays, rivers, and the Great Lakes.

Word of Mouth

Listen to what other anglers are saying. Word of mouth is one of the oldest methods for locating fish. Don't forget that the best anglers seldom whisper directions to their secret fishing holes.

The Thermocline

In some parts of the United States where seasonal cooling and warming trends affect lakes and ponds, the fish tend to seek a layer where summer temperatures range between 50 and 75 degrees. Known as the *thermocline*, this is the middle layer sandwiched between the top layer or *epilimnion*, which absorbs surface heat from the sun, and the bottom layer or *hypolimnion*, which is a few degrees colder than the thermocline and contains less oxygen needed by fish.

Because of its temperature, the thermocline provides the best habitat for fish and therefore is the best place to start looking for them during hot summer days. To find the thermocline, attach a water gauge thermometer to a line and lower it to specific depths. Record the temperature differences every five feet until you find 63 °F, a typical median temperature for the thermocline in a midwestern lake in late summer.

In winter, the cooling effect of land surrounding large bodies of water causes the thermocline to disappear and fish to scatter over depths spanning 60 feet.

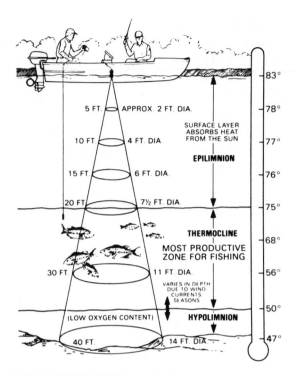

Figure 2.3. The thermocline is the layer of greatest interest to anglers because it provides the water temperature that most fish prefer. Here is an example of a stratified lake with water temperatures taken on August 10. Photo: Lowrance Electronics, Inc.

Electronic Fish Locators

It's a matter of physics that sound travels faster through water than it does through air (4,800 feet per second vs. 1,100 feet per second). At the end of World War I, scientists developed a device to convert electrical impulses into sound waves, which could be transmitted through water, echoed off the bottom and any object below the surface, received at the surface, and converted back into electrical impulses. Invented by British naval scientists and field-tested in 1921, it was originally called ASDIC, an acronym for Allied Submarine Detection Investigation Committee. They kept the device secret until World War II when Allied forces used it to track enemy submarines. It later became known as *sonar* in the U.S. Navy, short for sound, navigation, and ranging.

In 1957, the father and son team of Carl and Darrell Lowrance developed the first transistorized, high-frequency sonar that could be carried on board a small boat and used to locate underwater structures and individual fish.

At first the echo signals received by the Lowrance sonar instrument were indicated by a high-intensity neon bulb that was whirled at a constant speed behind a calibrated disc driven by a smooth, electric motor. Later, the Lowrance corporation of Tulsa, Oklahoma converted this technology so that the echo signals put out by a transducer on the bottom of a boat could be plotted on graph paper by a rotating stylus. The stylus marked a special type of paper as the paper rolled from one reel to another. This enabled anglers to chart the bottom of a lake while a boat was in motion.

An addition of a small computer led to another improvement of this paper graph recorder. With a computerized sonar graphic recorder, anglers can automatically set desired depths to scan an area for fish and structure; they also have the flexibility to pinpoint smaller objects such as baitfish and even plankton, the bottom link in a fish's food chain.

Because signals sent out by a transducer cover a cone-shaped area from the bottom of the boat to the bottom of the lake, any fish swimming through this cone will appear as hook-shaped marks on the graph

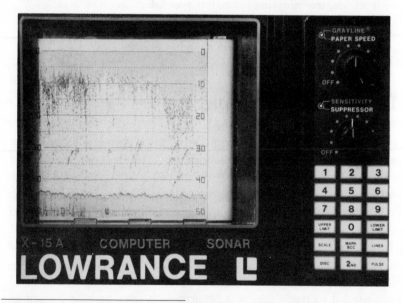

Figure 2.4.   Fish show up as hook-shaped marks on the paper of a graphic recorder.   Photo: Lowrance Electronics, Inc.

paper. Harder objects, such as rock bottoms and submerged stumps will appear darker on the graph paper than, for example, a mucky bottom or a weed bed. Subtle adjustments can be made in the sensitivity of the recorder and its gray line to make the different structures appear more obvious.

The advantage of a paper graph recorder is that the angler has a clear record of what it's like beneath the surface. During the 1970s, another technological advancement, the liquid crystal display, added a new twist to the fish-locating business. It allowed anglers to see a picture of the underwater world on a display terminal that changes as the boat travels over objects of different sensitivities.

Today's serious anglers are seldom without one of these fish-locating machines which have revolutionized the sport.

Figure 3.1. (opposite page) Choosing the right fly might make the difference between landing a trophy fish and coming home empty-handed. This king salmon fell for a green streamer that guide Tom Ugrin worked in a deep hole of the Eel River in California's Redwood Empire.
Photo: Keith Rogers

chapter 3

Bait

I always get a kick out of people who try to put three gobs of worms on their hooks, dragging behind a flasher, two minnows, and a spinner. They usually catch nothing but twisted line. Once in a while, a bait fisherman will offer the fish a smorgasbord of worms and minnows and catch a big one; but that's a rare occurrence. These anglers are people who can't make up their minds whether to fish with lures or bait.

Worms/Nightcrawlers

Let's consider the world's most classic bait: worms, particularly night-crawlers. No freshwater game fish can pass up a nightcrawler dangled in front of its nose. When rigged properly, a live nightcrawler is ir-resistible to trout, walleye, bass, pike, muskie, catfish, rough fishes, and most anadromous species (i.e., fish that can live in both fresh and salt water).

From their outward appearance, nightcrawlers have three body parts: head, collar, and tail or foot portion. Anglers typically thread night-crawlers on a long-shank hook by sticking the point in at its collar and running the shank through the worm's tail portion. Most fish attack the tail where it dangles over the point of the hook. A clever fish will hit with such force that it sometimes rips off the tail; then it's time to bait up and try again.

When fishing in deep weed beds for trout, you can inject nightcrawlers with air so their tails float above the weeds and can be spotted by a trout cruising for a meal.

Anglers also fish with nightcrawlers right off the bottom using a tight line, leaving about a 20-inch leader between the hook and the sinker. The same effect can be achieved by tying the hook 20 inches above a split shot or several split shots at the end of the line.

Nightcrawlers can be drifted off the back of a boat or fished below a bobber. Use a slip-type bobber for fishing deep holes off the bottom. A cherry bobber is adequate for shallow water and ideal for lobbing nightcrawlers to the edge of bushes.

Nightcrawler hunting was a ritual for my brother and me on the eve-ning before we planned to fish a nearby lake or gravel quarry. We'd water the lawn and bushes. Later, when night fell, we'd return with flashlights to see who had the quicker hand for grabbing crawlers as they lay with half their bodies sticking from holes in the damp ground.

Insects and Larvae

Natural baits from the surrounding environment appeal the most to fish. Grasshoppers and crickets from nearby fields make excellent baits for panfish and trout. These insects are hooked through their hard body, leaving their legs and wings free to twitch. Grubs or beetle larvae are natural baits throughout the United States. They work well on panfish and perch and are hooked like worms.

Frogs

Small frogs and salamanders, hooked either through the lips or thighs so that they swim freely, make tempting appetizers for large, black bass. A good way to attract bass when fishing from the shoreline of a lake or farm pond is to hook a small diving frog through its lips and place it about 12 feet below a slip bobber.

I remember one morning when I sat on shoreline with no nightcrawlers in my bucket; I baited my hook with a frog which I snatched from its perch on a grass-covered rock. I stuck a hook through the lips of the fist-sized frog and let it swim around at a depth of 13 feet, just a toss off the shoreline formed by a steep embankment. Minutes later, a 4-pound largemouth bass latched onto that frog and caused my slip-bobber to disappear like a pencil fading to the bottom of the lake. When the bobber had stayed down long enough for the bass to swallow the frog, I told my partner, "Either the frog ate that bass or the bass is a lot fatter now." Then I raised my rod tip high and let that bass feel my hook in its throat. To paraphrase one popular adage: "A frog in the hand is worth a bass on the bank."

Crayfish

Crayfish (also known as crawdads), those lobster-like critters that inhabit lakes, ditches, and reservoirs in central and southern states, are natural food for bass, catfish, and other predators. Soft-shelled crayfish are preferred over the hard-shelled variety, although both types catch fish.

Crayfish are hooked live by inserting the point of a single hook at the bottom of the segmented tail, threading it toward its belly. The barb should protrude from its underside. Some anglers snip the pinchers off crayfish and fish them like large shrimp. Others use just the tail of a crayfish, shucked from its armor-like shell and threaded on a hook.

Ray Easley caught the largest Florida-strain largemouth bass in the last 50 years with a live crayfish. He landed that fish while drifting

Lake Casitas in California in the spring of 1980. The lunker weighed 21 pounds, 3 ounces.

Minnows

Minnows can be rigged on a hook in numerous ways. Smaller crappie minnows can be hooked through the lips; this method is not recommended when going after large panfish capable of ripping apart the tender lips of a minnow.

Larger minnows should be used for larger fish. They can be hooked through the meaty part near their dorsal fins or by a *mooching rig*. A mooching rig is a two-hook setup on a monofilament leader. The bottom hook is stationary while the top hook is tied so it slides on the leader and can be adjusted to fit the length of a baitfish. This way, large baitfish such as sucker minnows, sculpin (staghorn and riffle), and mudsuckers can be rigged with a hook under their chins and one along their lateral lines near the tail.

Artificial Bait

There's no greater challenge in the sport of fishing than to convince a wild game fish to strike at an artificial bait, whether it's a fly, spinner, plug, spoon, jig, or plastic worm. When it comes to artificial bait, often referred to as *hardware* in the angler's world, rules don't apply. Commonsense and ingenuity are worth at least 50 rules in this game.

I watched a guy carve a shallow-running plug from a broomhandle one day and paint it just like a large minnow. He said it caught fish. I believed him and went to the tackle store to buy a plug that looked just like his broomhandle plug. When I got home, I took a pair of needle-nose pliers and pinched the nose eyelet, leaving enough room to push a pencil lead through it. Then, I bent that eyelet up slightly and to one side. This made the plug skitter as I reeled it through the water. It would swim along and then suddenly zigzag to the right or left.

I caught bass after bass with this particular plug because it had the right action. I found that reeling faster as I raised my rod tip toward the end of my retrieves often angered fish into striking. Big fish don't

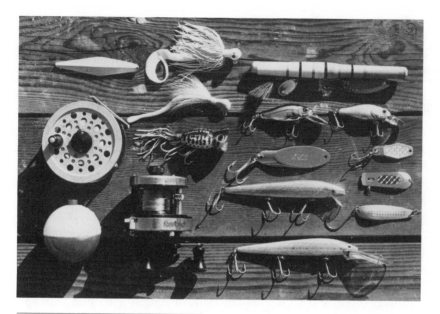

Figure 3.2.   Lures, bobbers, and reels come in an assortment of shapes, sizes, and colors.   Photo: Thomas Ovalle

like to let smaller baitfish get away, especially dumb-looking plastic ones that swim as if they can see.

Fish strike by instinct. A spinner purring at the surface or a spoon fluttering toward the bottom arouses the curiosity of fish. Thinking it's a free meal, they come to investigate. That's when to stick them with a hook.

Color

Fish strike out of hunger, anger, and excitement. Certain colors excite certain fish in certain lakes and rivers. The color of the water and the sky also play a role in what color of lure an angler should select from a tackle box. Many times the color represents the pattern of a baitfish that they feed on.

My father always told me that if you are fishing an unfamiliar lake and don't know what the fish are hitting on, try a Flatfish lure. The one with the green-and-yellow frog pattern works best.

Lures come in all shapes, sizes, and prices. The ones that have been proven to catch the most fish usually cost more because of high demand and low supply. Usually, if someone catches a big fish on, for example, a pink-spotted fliptail daddy junior, everyone suddenly wants a pink-spotted fliptail daddy junior.

Most of the time, it doesn't matter what you're using as long as it resembles what the fish are looking for and it's presented to them properly with the right speed, drift, and action.

I've discovered a few tips about color patterns. Always have something black in your tackle box. Black surface plugs, poppers, and the like put out good silhouettes when used at night or during the twilight hours. Black is also good for lures fished in deep holes, along shady shorelines and hidden structures. Black is also an excellent color for plastic worms, flies that are patterned after leeches, and minnow-imitation plugs when they are fished in cold rivers and reservoirs.

Silver is one of those colors that fish strike because it resembles flashy baitfish. Anything from white to metallic blue lures will often have the same effect, depending on the color of the water and the sky at the time. Water that appears blue-hued in deep lakes of western United States, New England, and the mountains are good places to try blue lures. Bright silver, I've learned, seems to produce results in chalky or muddy water.

Shades of pink and red work well as lure colors for trout and salmon because it's the natural color of their eggs. Select the intensity of the color based on the stream depending on whether it's clearing or becoming muddier. Use brighter patterns for muddier streams. As the water begins to clear, select shades that are closer to pink instead of flame red.

When fly fishing streams for salmon, there's a rule to remember with pink-and-orange fuzz balls known as "glow bugs." When drifting these salmon-egg imitations, if your line suddenly stops, pull back in the opposite direction and plant your boots. If it's a salmon that's as big as a sack of potatoes, be ready to plow your own rows right there in the river. King or chinook salmon strike certain flies lightly. The big, hook-snouted male chinooks will gingerly pick up a fuzz ball that looks like roe and try to put it under a rock or pile of gravel. That's when your line stops and you should pull back.

On the one hand, it's amazing how lightly those big chinooks can strike. On the other hand, I've seen them try to destroy a spinner or spoon that twirled by their noses because it angered them.

A red-and-white spoon is vital to northern pike anglers who are fishing natural lakes in and around the Great Lakes. Red-and-white surface plugs also work well for bass and pike.

Green and brown are crayfish colors. They make excellent choices for crank baits (deep-diving action lures) and plastic worms. Use brown, purple, or motor-oil colors for jigs and plastic worms.

White spinner baits with white or white-and-gray skirts attract shad-eating fish when these spinners are cranked at a steady pace from a shoreline to a boat or parallel to a shoreline. I've found this combination to be most effective in the spring and early summer months.

Yellow and green patterns apply to northern waters, eastern lakes, southern marshes, and gravel quarries where frogs and barred, yellow perch live. Remember that pike pluggers should try perch patterns.

Spinners

By definition, a spinner is a lure with a propeller or spoon-like blade that flutters on a wire shaft as it's pulled through the water. The spinning action of the blade antagonizes fish into striking.

Spinners come in an assortment of sizes, not necessarily proportional to the size of the fish that strike them. Some spinners are attached to lead-headed, skirted jigs. They add a minnow-like effect to the lure, enhanced by the spinning action of the blades. A simple spinner can be constructed of small-gauged wire, an egg-shaped spoon with a hole drilled near the center of the small end, some beads, and bucktail or squirrel fur that appears lifelike when wet.

Spinners can be cast or trolled. They should be trolled slowly and with a snap-swivel to prevent twisting the line. Small, Rocky Mountain-type spinners, which are effective for trout, have also produced nice walleyes from murky midwestern lakes. Spinners as an attachment to jigs or plastic grubs are referred to as *bushwackers* because of their ability to travel through sparse weedbeds without snagging.

A series of large spinners threaded on heavy leader material and trolled in front of a nightcrawler are called *attractors*. They cause commotion in the water as they're trolled, arousing curiosity of nearby fish that come to investigate and are essentially attracted to the bait.

Plugs

If I accepted a challenge to go to a lake in the middle of the woods but could take only one lure with me, it would probably be a plug. Plugs

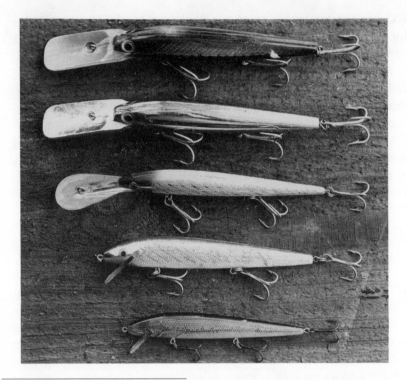

Figure 3.3. A bass plug's action and depth depend partly on the shape of its lip.   Photo: Michael Macor

are lures that have a body or jointed body, usually made of some type of buoyant wood or plastic. They are connected to a line at an eyelet either located in the nose of a plug or on the top above its eyes. They usually have treble hooks instead of single hooks, which add to their hooking power and add action to the plug. Most plugs have a lip that, depending on its size and shape, causes it to dig through the water like a baitfish swimming or a frog or crawdad taking off.

Plugs can be worked or trolled. This means that plugs can be either cast and reeled in, which is called "working" the hole, or trolled, which means to drag them behind a moving boat. In the latter case, the speed of the boat determines how much action the plug has. These techniques will be discussed in more detail in chapter 6.

Subsurface plugs have smaller lips than deep-divers. They are designed for fishing in shallow lakes or rivers or when fish are detected feeding at or near the surface. Subsurface plugs can be cast and retrieved immediately at different speeds. Or, they can be tossed near a structure and allowed to sit for a few seconds before the caster twitches his rod-tip causing a skitterish action to the plug as it takes off in a series of spurts that fade into a slow, steady retrieve.

In this scenario, a fish hears the plug plop at the surface. The plug is allowed to sit for a bit so that the fish below can locate it using the full extent of its peripheral vision. Having found it, the fish waits for a second move from the plug before it investigates. Then as the plug appears to be getting away like an injured minnow, the game fish attacks it in an explosive strike that usually sprays water into the air. Subsurface plugs make for exciting fishing. A good subsurface plug is one that's been knocked by fish so many times that its paint is chipped and scarred with teeth marks.

Another type of subsurface plug is a flat, bone-shaped lure. Its lip is actually a gradual taper of its body. These plugs, known as Ikes, Flatfish, or Hot Shots can be let out into a current behind a boat about 40 to 60 feet downstream. The technique is called *back oaring* or *back rowing*, because the person who is rowing the boat controls the placement of the lures in the stream by rowing backwards, thus holding the boat in the current while the lures wiggle from the water rushing around them. The helmsman gradually allows the boat to move downstream, working the river from side to side while the plugs wander through holes and over boulders. No snap-swivel is required for these subsurface plugs. Snap swivels have a tendency to kill the plug's action, although a split-ring—a small double ring about the diameter of a pencil with a gap where the ring can be attached to a lure—or loose-noose knot will keep the line from twisting. The loose-noose knot will be discussed in chapter 5.

Another technique for working topwater, artificial baits is to cast them near structures, over weedbeds, or around lily pads. Allow them to sit long enough for you to take your hat off, scratch your head, and do it again. Then, twitch the lure before the retrieve. Make it pop across the water if twitching doesn't produce results. Have patience when fishing the surface but always be ready to set the hook.

Reel up slack line after each controlled jerk. More hookups are lost when fish strike a plug during slack line than when the line is kept taut. Anglers should experiment with different techniques on the retrieve.

Plugs make ideal lures because they have more room for variety in both color and action. They can be painted like baitfish or bees. Some, like poppers, can be equipped with rubber-tentacled skirts. Others can be flecked with glitter or painted in scale-like patterns. A few topwater plugs even have small propellers or spinner blades on their tails and noses to add more commotion at the surface.

When it comes to selecting plugs or any lure from a tackle box, remember to choose one with eyes painted or etched near the nose. Fish readily identify their prey by the eyes it has. There aren't too many eyeless baitfish swimming around. Grasshoppers, frogs, crayfish, and most of a fish's natural bait have noticeable eyes with the exception of night-crawlers and worm-like critters. If the lure you want to use doesn't have eyes, get a small paintbrush and some contrasting paint and paint some on.

Flies

Fly fishing is a sport in itself. It is not necessary, however, to use a fly rod to cast flies although that is the most effective way of presenting an artificial bug to a fish. Spin casters can thread monofilament line through the sleeve of a clear plastic bubble. The sleeve is adjustable so that the bubble can be filled with water to add the weight needed for casting and to give the fly a proper drift in the current.

Generally, flies are much smaller than most lures. They are tied of different, lightweight materials: feathers, fur, thread, yarn, plastic

Figure 3.4. Fly patterns range from streamers to nymphs, most of which imitate various life cycles of bugs and baitfish.   Photo: Michael Macor

strands, and tinsel, usually on a small hook. The materials appear life-like when wet, giving the fly a flexible appearance that's in constant motion.

There are two types of flies, wet and dry. Dry flies are treated with a sticky, liquid dressing that keeps them afloat. Wet flies sink and can be weighted to sink even faster and deeper in a current by wrapping thin strips of lead parallel to the hook shank.

Large flies, known as streamers, are typically made of different colored feathers either from a chicken or game bird. They imitate bait-fish, not insects, and can be trolled in a lake or cast upon a river for large trout, bass, and pike.

The art of tying flies resides in an angler's ability to shape these materials into the five parts of an artificial fly: head, wings, body, tail, and hackle. Hackle, the long slender feathers from the neck of a rooster, add character to a fly. Bristle-like hackle made from animal fur or stiffer bird feathers give dry flies more buoyancy when arranged so that they stick out at right angles to a hook.

Depending on the type of insect hatching on the water at the time, the materials are arranged to match that stage in an insect's growth. Flies can be tied to look like an insect in the larval or adult stage. Wing-less insects are called nymphs, which are actually immature aquatic in-sects. Common flies used by trout fishermen include stone flies, May flies, and brightly colored nymphs.

Shad flies, so named for their popularity in catching American shad that migrate from the oceans to rivers and streams on the East and West Coasts, are designed with small strips of lead wrapped around the hook's shank. The lead, along with eyes made from a pair of beads snipped from a key chain, makes it drift deep and upright in a stream to keep the fly at the depth where shad strike.

A dry fly simulates either a dead or live insect and is allowed to drift in the current. A wet fly, on the other hand, is worked in by an angler who draws it smoothly through the current in a series of short, rhythmic tugs. Each fly fisherman has his or her own style of working a fly. Stick with whatever technique works and feels most comfortable.

Jigs

No angler's tackle box is complete without some type of jig. Jigs are perhaps the simplest of lures, consisting of a single, long-shanked hook and a skirt or flexible rubber or plastic body. Typically, jigs have heads made of lead or heavy metal. They are sized according to fractions of an ounce. Larger jigs weighing more than an ounce work well in extremely fast water or for trolling in combination with action lures on wire-framed spreader rigs.

Jigs are worked by casting and retrieving at a fairly rapid pace after they have sunk to a desired depth. Or, they can be bounced up and down in a stationary position. This is known as *vertical jigging*. The most popular colors are solid white or solid yellow. Brown or black jigs are effective for jigging throughout the United States. A jig that has a head that appears to have been sliced is called a *dart*, and is designed for drifting rivers.

Spoons

An old-timer fishing from the bank told me one slow afternoon that a shiny spoon tossed into the whitewater below the falls of Cataract Lake in Indiana would bring the smallmouth bass out of hiding. He was right.

Spoons are heavy hunks of metal, shaped like the end of a teaspoon. They usually have a small hole drilled at one end where a slip-ring is placed to attach it to a line. A second hole at the other end is drilled for a hook, single, dual, or treble. Some spoons have hooks welded directly to the spoon. Some are painted red and white and are dented at one end to produce a certain wiggle. These are excellent for northern pike fishing.

Spoons can be reeled in directly or allowed to bump along the bottom of a swift river. Some have smooth shiny surfaces. Others have a hammered, scale-like appearance.

Spoons are ideal artificial bait for vertical jigging along underwater shelves and drop-offs. The technique here is to raise the rod and let the spoon flutter to the bottom as it falls, repeating this action over and over again. They might look like wounded minnows to lurking bass or pike.

Plastic Worms

Artificial worms that jiggle and loaf through the water are perhaps the most common bait used by professional black bass anglers. Though

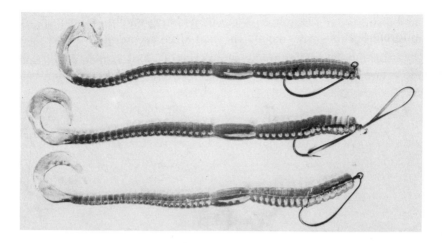

Figure 3.5. Plastic worms can be made weedless by using one of three hooking methods. Photo: Michael Macor

sometimes called rubber worms, they are actually made of a flexible plastic that is translucent but shaded with color.

The action in plastic worms is in their tails. The angler flips the worm and the tail flutters, tempting game fish to pick it up in their mouths and run with it. Sometimes they are attached to a silver-colored propeller/bead arrangement that is thought to attract fish. Though this works, I have found that a torpedo-shaped piece of lead weighing about 3/8 ounce positioned at the nose of a plastic worm gives adequate casting weight and provides better action.

A single hook is all that's needed for this set up. It can be made weedless by a thin wire, rubber band, or preferably by inserting the hook's point through a plastic worm's nose, back out, and finally embedded at the collar of the plastic worm. The worm should appear flat with no point showing. This method of rigging is called "Texas style" because of its popularity in south central United States.

Generally, plastic worms are about five to seven inches long, but shorter ones are effective for simulating crawdad action. Longer worms are cast and allowed to sink; then they are twitched or creeped along the bottom. Many times a bass will hit a plastic worm as it falls. Catfish have also been known to attack them.

For crawdad action, use a brown, green, or combination-colored worm. Colors are mixed by melting solid-colored worms in a pan and pouring them as desired into a mold. A flat, paddle tail produces a floppy

action similar to a crawdad taking off from the lake floor. The action
is produced by casting the worm, letting it settle to the bottom, and
then shaking the rodtip rapidly as it is raised. Slack is then reeled and
the action is repeated. This is called *doodling* a worm.

Figure 4.1.　(opposite page) This 43-pound striped bass was caught by the
author downstream of where the Sacramento and San Joaquin rivers meet in
California.　Photo: Randy Becker

chapter
4

Freshwater
game fish

Like neighbors in an underwater city, fish belong to families, each with different physical traits and preferences for living conditions. Their habitats are their homes. Fishery biologists have given each type of fish a scientific name, usually a Latin word that describes it (or a Latin word made from the discoverer's name), and designates its general family grouping; this is followed by a smaller or genus grouping and a species designation.

For example, rainbow trout have the scientific name *Salmonidae Salmo gairdneri*. *Salmonidae* refers to the family of trouts, chars, and salmon. The genus name, *Salmo*, pertains to a smaller trout-type grouping. It is followed by the species designation, *gairdneri*, which differentiates rainbows from other trouts such as golden trout (*Salmo aquabonita*) or cutthroat trout (*Salmo clarki*). A special type of cutthroat trout, the coast cutthroat, a native to northern California, has a genus, species, and subspecies name, *Salmo clarki clarki*.

Not counting carp and numerous other rough fishes (those with many small bones that are generally not appealing to eat) U.S. freshwater species can be lumped into categories of bass, trout, panfish, catfish, and pike or northern game fishes. Technically, bass such as black bass and most panfish are all members of the sunfish family. But for purposes of sport fish identification, I separate the bass from all other sunfishes to allow for general differences in size and angling techniques.

Many anglers rate the Florida-strain subspecies as the smartest and most difficult of all the black bass to catch. Florida-strain largemouths seem to live longer than northern largemouths. For this reason they are often bigger fish, sometimes weighing more than 20 pounds. Florida-strain bass prefer relatively warm, shallow water instead of the deep and shallow habitats of northern largemouths and have about 70 scales on their lateral line whereas the same scales on northern largemouth bass number about 65.

Fish Anatomy

An experienced angler becomes familiar with the anatomy of the different fish families. Some terms often referred to when identifying fish include fins, scales, line markings, rays, and mouth features. All fish have some type of fin arrangement that helps them swim and maneuver. The fins on the top or back of a fish are its dorsal fins. Dorsal fins usually consist of sharp-pointed spines, each separated by a film-like layer of skin. Spines are a defensive mechanism which allow the fish to stick its predators. Fins without spines are supported by soft-structured rays. Other fins associated with various fishes include the pectoral fin, located behind and on each side of the head of a fish; the pelvic or ventral fin, located on its underside; and the anal fin, located between the pelvic fin and the tail. The tail is called a caudal fin.

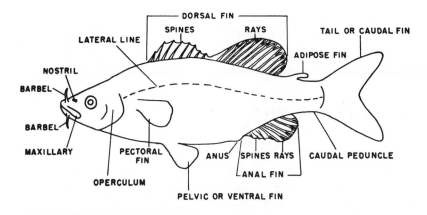

Figure 4.2. This hypothetical fish has the physical features that anglers should be acquainted with. Not all of the features are found on any one kind of fish.   Photo: California Department of Fish and Game

Another characteristic of most freshwater fish is that they have large, bony plates on the sides of their heads. These plates have flexible edges for protecting the gills, a fish's breathing mechanism, and for letting oxygen-bearing water enter the gill system.

A fish's lateral line extends from the back of its gill plate to the center of its tail. It allows a fish to sense pressure and currents and enables it to detect other fish and objects moving through the water. It is a major physical characteristic that is necessary for fish to find prey in total darkness. Although fish have no ear openings, they can sense vibrations, the source of sound, in the open water. Catfish and some types of minnows do have a small chain of bones next to their swim bladders, like the inner ear bones near a human's eardrum, for detecting some sound waves. But for the most part, fish rely on their whole body structure to act as ears.

Like most other animals, fish have eyes and nostrils for seeing and smelling. Some fish, usually bottom feeders, have fleshy, whisker-like barbels that aid in their feeling and sensing abilities.

Fish also have lips, jaws, and a vent located on their underside for waste excretion and spawning. Some freshwater fish such as pike have sharp, pointed teeth. Others like bass have tiny, brush-like teeth on the inside of their upper and lower lips. Most fish have some variation of a tongue.

Except for color differences or alterations in the jaws or head size of a certain fish, a fish's sex can otherwise be distinguished by the underside bulge of female fish during spawning season. Even then, male and female fish often can't be distinguished unless they are cleaned for eating purposes.

Anadromous Fish

The gills of some fishes allow them to live in both fresh and salt water. Fish with this ability are called anadromous and include ocean-going species like Atlantic salmon, steelhead, chinook or king salmon, sockeye, and a few large-scaled fish such as striped bass, American shad, and tarpon.

As adults these anadromous fish swim up coastal rivers to spawn. Their hatch begins its life in the river. The young fish eventually swim to the ocean where they fatten up on smaller sea life and plankton until they are tough enough to return to the same stream where they hatched. Biologists have concluded that king salmon know how to return to the very creek where they began life through their acute sense of smell. King salmon remember the scent of the stream where they were hatched. Biologists call this characteristic a *scent fingerprint* which endures little change over the years and distinguishes that particular stream from all others.

With this homing ability, king salmon travel thousands of miles in the ocean for three or four years before returning to the mouth of the same river. During this time they feed voraciously on anchovies, herring, and smaller fishes until, in just three years' time, some chinooks have

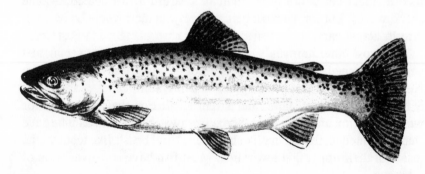

Figure 4.3. A steelhead is a rainbow trout that makes several runs from the ocean to spawn in the stream where it hatched. Photo: California Department of Fish and Game.

grown from a few ounces to the 30- and 40-pound lunkers that entice sportfishermen from Alaska to California.

Unfortunately, king salmon die after the hens (females) have dropped their eggs and the bucks (males) have sprayed their milt, initiating the spawning cycle all over again. Steelhead live this cycle several times before dying after an upstream spawning run. Atlantic salmon, as well, may spawn more than once before they die, their bodies tattered from negotiating the rocky rivers to return to the place where their lives began.

American shad, like salmon, stay at sea for about four years thriving on plankton before they begin a trek to the gravel bars of East and West Coast rivers. They swim a starvation journey against the currents, their stomachs decreasing in size as their bodies become heavy with roe. The smaller male fish arrive at the spawning grounds first. Females, some weighing six or seven pounds, follow days later to deposit their eggs and die.

Striped bass are fast becoming America's top game fish because of their inherent ocean-run instincts that dictate their appetites and supremacy in reservoirs where man has transplanted them. Landlocked striped bass, whose return to the sea has been blocked by dams and state water projects, have thrived well in their freshwater environments. However, at least two problems have developed because of this: Their instincts drive them to devour other freshwater sport fish, hampering the existence of those species; and, because their eggs are heavier than the still waters of most reservoirs, the eggs sink to the bottom and become infertile. Striped bass need the current of a river to suspend their eggs and carry them along for a while until fertilization has a chance to happen. Unlike the native black basses, landlocked striped bass must be continually restocked whether it be through a fish and game program or accidentally through manmade waterways.

In 1879 biologists transplanted the striped bass, a native to East Coast waters, from New Jersey's Navesink River by the transcontinental railroad to the Carquinez Straits of the Sacramento River system on the West Coast. The successful planting blossomed into a commercial fishery in California by 1890 and set the pace for future transplants of anadromous fish, some that brought populations of Pacific king salmon to the Great Lakes and others that put millions of striped bass in lakes and reservoirs in some 30 states.

The Basses

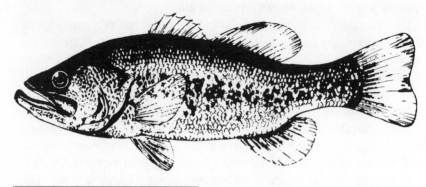

Figure 4.4. Largemouth bass. World record: 22 pounds, 4 ounces,
caught in Montgomery Lake, Georgia, by George W. Perry on June 2, 1932.
Photo: California Department of Fish and Game

Largemouth Bass

Largemouth bass (*Micropterus salmoides*), commonly known in the
angling world as bucketmouths, big mouths, or black bass, are found
throughout the nation's contiguous 48 states and have been introduced
into Hawaiian inland waters. Strictly a freshwater fish, it is one of the
most popular game fish across America, not because of its size but rather
for the challenge involved in outsmarting one. They prefer warm water
(65° or warmer) but can survive cold winters in ice-covered lakes as
their bodies become lethargic and their appetites diminish when the temperature drops below 50 degrees.

Largemouth bass are attracted by plugs, spinners, flies, plastic worms,
jigs, and poppers. Live minnows, grubs, and nightcrawlers suffice for
live bait options when seeking the elusive largemouth.

They spawn in the spring as water temperatures rise. State fish and
game biologists estimate that the females lay between 2,000 and 40,000
eggs. The young grow to nearly 12 inches by age two.

Introduction of Florida-strain bass into lakes near San Diego in 1959
has resulted in several fish approaching George Perry's world-record
catch. Casitas Reservoir along the coast near Ventura, California, has
produced two world-class largemouth bass: an 11-pound fish caught
on 2-pound test line and Ray Easley's whopping 21-pound, 3-ounce
Florida strain which fell for a live crawdad on March 4, 1980.

Two Georgia lakes, Allatoona near Atlanta and Lake Chatuge, have
produced world-class largemouths larger than 16 pounds.

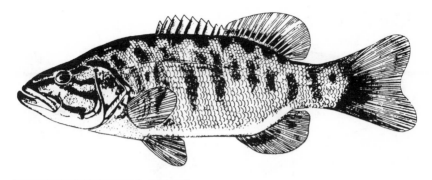

Figure 4.5.   Smallmouth bass. World record: 11 pounds, 15 ounces, caught in Dale Hollow Lake, Kentucky, by David L. Hayes on July 9, 1955. Photo: California Department of Fish and Game

Smallmouth Bass

The largemouth's closest cousin, the smallmouth bass (*Micropterus dolomieui*), is a smaller species by comparison of world records. Yet, it is a tenacious fighter and a prized catch in any angler's creel. Generally lighter in color, ranging from dark shades of bronze to green as opposed to the darker olive appearance of the largemouth, smallmouths as their name implies have smaller mouths. The upper jaw of a smallmouth bass intersects its lower jaw at a point on an imaginary line extending from the center of its eye. A largemouth's upper jaw, however, extends beyond its eye and its dorsal fins are separated by a deep notch between the dorsals of a smallmouth. Markings also differ between the two fishes with a smallmouth having vertical bars while a largemouth has a dark lateral band that runs from its tail to its gill plate.

Smallmouth bass prefer rocky structures in swift streams and pools close to boulder-lined banks of meandering rivers. They are native to eastern states yet are widespread throughout the United States and southern Canada.

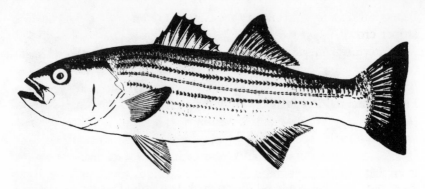

Figure 4.6.   Striped bass. World record: 59 pounds, 12 ounces, caught in the Colorado River, Arizona, by Frank W. Smith on May 26, 1977.
Photo: California Department of Fish and Game

Striped Bass

Popularity of fishing for striped bass (*Morone saxitilis*) is fast approaching the level of enthusiasm that anglers have for black bass fishing. In fact, many bass anglers have stuffed their black bass plugs in a forgotten corner of their tackle boxes and opted for the challenge of striped bass plugging, a feat best accomplished with lures that look like sawed-off broom handles rather than 3-inch hunks of mechanized tinsel.

In a historical perspective, striped bass fishing is fairly new to the freshwater/landlocked scene, though stripers were caught by many an Indian as well as the Pilgrims who intercepted their annual spawning migration to rivers along the Atlantic seaboard.

A voracious, opportunistic feeder, the freshwater striped bass is primarily an open water fish which now thrives in rivers, canals, and reservoirs in three-fifths of the United States. Unlike black bass and other sunfishes, the landlocked striped bass grows more rapidly than an ocean-going striped bass; some landlocked stripers measure 18 inches after the second year. Fishery biologists have found that sea-run stripers, on the other hand, average 10 inches at age 2. A 36-inch sea-run striper will be about 10 to 12 years old and weigh 19 pounds. By comparison, a landlocked striped bass with an adequate supply of forage fish to support its unending appetite can gain as much as five pounds per year and weigh 21-1/2 pounds at age 6.

In some lakes, however, such as Lake Powell in Arizona, the striped bass is its own worst enemy; its domination of that sprawling, canyon reservoir has resulted in too many stripers that are too lean for their age. Lake Powell does have its share of 30- and 40-pound fish, but state fishery officials in 1986 encouraged anglers to trim down Lake Powell's striper crowd.

As previously mentioned, striped bass are not native to the West Coast, rather they were transplanted to Carquinez Straits near San Francisco Bay in 1879. U.S. fisheries biologist, Livingston Stone, and California Fish Commissioner, Stephen Throckmorton, seined 162 small stripers from New Jersey's Navesink River during the summer of that year and arranged for their speedy delivery aboard the transcontinental railroad. In 1882, they made a second planting of 300 fish at lower Suisun Bay; from that grew a population that totaled millions, perhaps 10 million adult fish. It supported a commercial fishery in the early decades of the 1900s.

As time progressed, West Coast striped bass ranged from Monterey, California to Coos Bay, Oregon where a second population flourished in the Umpqua River. They have been reportedly caught as far north on the Pacific Coast as Oak Park, Washington.

The first successful landlocked striped bass fishery evolved in South Carolina after the Santee and Cooper rivers were dammed in 1941. A hatchery established there provided the seed for many landlocked bass fisheries in other states at a time when the federal government and the State of California plotted a water transport system that literally sucked the lifeblood out of what once was an abundant population of migratory bass. The federal and state water projects whittled the millions of adult striped bass that spawned in the delta and upper reaches of the San Joaquin and Sacramento rivers to a figure that has been debated as being less than 1 million since 1985. When adult fish returned to the delta to spawn during a period from the 1950s until the mid-1970s, billions of young striped bass fry, eggs, and larvae evaded fish screens and were sucked into the intake pumps that filled the southward canals. Many young fish died from such abuse but millions infiltrated California reservoirs and survived in the canals themselves, unable to return to the sea and spawn in their natural habitat. The result was a substantial decline in the migratory population, a fact that sportsmen's clubs, namely the California Striped Bass Association and the United Anglers of California, have sought to reverse by convincing the state government to curtail pumping during April, May, and June. They successfully advocated the sale of striped bass stamps to support a hatchery for restocking and studying stripers in the delta and landlocked environments.

Also called the striper, linesider, greenhead, and rock, striped bass vary in color from silver or steel-blue to olive-green with seven or eight black stripes. A striper has the same number of lines on each of its sides. Ocean-run bass tend to have jet-black features with silvery sides and white undersides. Landlocked striped bass, having never been in salt water, are often more blue-green in appearance with occasional flecks of turquoise dispersed in their scaled, black lines.

Landlocked stripers have adapted to a diet of freshwater shad, either gizzard or threadfin, and they are fond of other smaller baitfishes such as Mississippi silversides, riffle sculpin, staghorn sculpin, mudsuckers, and large shiners. They have been known to eat herring, anchovies, and other saltwater baits trolled or still-fished in freshwater. They are quite fond of many native inland sport fish including rainbow trout and largemouth and smallmouth bass.

Landlocked stripers will herd schools of baitfish that are suspended in a lake, corral them in a cove or surround them near underwater structures, and slaughter them in a frothy, tail-slapping frenzy at the surface. For this reason stripers readily strike shallow-running, subsurface plugs. They are "suckers" for fly streamers, spoons, and lead-headed jigs and will hit crayfish, shrimp, clams, and redworms.

A 12-pound female striped bass can produce over a million pea-green colored eggs after spawning in waters with temperatures between 61 and 69 °F. Only sporadic spawning occurs in most landlocked settings; but flowing waters of the Santee-Cooper system in South Carolina, the Lake Havasu-Colorado River system on the Arizona-California border, and Lake Meade in Nevada are all believed to yield conditions conducive for landlocked bass reproduction.

Other than Frank Smith's landlocked world record of nearly 60 pounds, Kentucky's Lake Cumberland produced a world-record 45-pound, 8-ounce striped bass which was caught by Walter Lilly in 1978 on 8-pound test line. In addition, Smith Mountain Lake in Virginia and Flint River, Georgia are in the books as having yielded world-record stripers for certain line classes.

The top, fly rod world record was a 19-pound, 4-ounce landlocked bass taken from All American Canal in California in 1982.

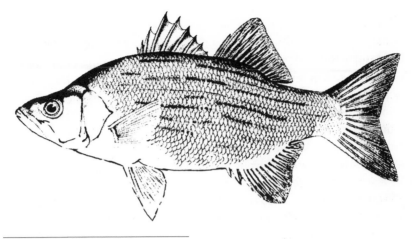

Figure 4.7. White bass. World record: 5 pounds, 9 ounces, caught in the Colorado River, Texas, by David S. Cordill on March 31, 1977.
Photo: California Department of Fish and Game

White Bass/Yellow Bass

Two other freshwater bass species resemble the striped bass but are much smaller by comparison. White bass, found in the Mississippi and Ohio river drainages and in three south central lakes are hard-hitting, fast-multiplying panfish.

Yellow bass are similar in appearance to white bass but they have golden yellow sides and three of seven stripes are below their lateral lines. The all-tackle world record yellow bass was caught from Lake Monroe, Indiana, by Donald L. Stalker on March 27, 1977. The fish weighed 2 pounds, 4 ounces.

White bass that were introduced into California's fishery fared well; illegal transplants of the species into lakes that empty into the San Joaquin River have alarmed biologists to a potential disaster. They fear that white bass could infiltrate the San Joaquin River and eventually the Sacramento River where cross-breeding with migratory striped bass could happen, resulting in a runted population of ocean-going stripers.

This linesided hybrid, the whiterock bass, does exist in Georgia's Savannah River where fishermen have caught some bigger than 20 pounds. The whiterock bass is actually a cross between a female striped bass and a male white bass. It is distinguished from the striper by its broken lines and smaller head.

Trout

The trout family is a colorful assortment of what idealists consider to be the fisherman's perfect fish. It is primarily a class of bug eaters, each with a passion for fighting and a physique as dynamic as a well-trained athlete. Trout are sleek-looking fish with a passion for jumping as they try to shake hooks. They have small scales and a skin-like appearance. They are designed for the environment of a river, stream, or lake. Studies have shown that trout respond to colors, particularly red and shades of red ranging to light pink.

Salmon, the family head of the trouts, are very responsive to the color of their own eggs, also known as roe. They instinctively pick up roe in their mouths as it drifts in spawning streams. Depending on the color of the stream, these big king salmon will readily hit *egg pattern* flies presented along a proper drift. A salmon fisherman chooses the shade of red that fits the condition.

Trouts are flashing specimens of blue and rose hues. Some have deep-red dots, speckled on a moss green background. Anadromous trouts are like silver dollars fresh from a mint. Their backs are dark, deep shades of black, aqua, and turquoise. They have keen eyesight and an acute sense of smell. Like most other fishes they respond to underwater vibrations. A bug twitching at the surface arouses their appetites as do grasshoppers.

Trout hear through their skin, particularly along the lateral line which picks up vibrations through rows of mucus-filled scales.

In native fish, their meat ranges in color from pale pink to deep red. Sockeye salmon have the reddest meat of trout members.

Salmon are essentially anadromous trouts that begin life in fresh streams and journey to the ocean where they spend years fattening up for a return journey to the very stream where they were hatched.

A steelhead is no different from an ocean-run rainbow trout. They are generally bigger than freshwater rainbows but the two are similar in appearance.

Figure 4.8.   Les Anderson (right) caught the world's largest member of
the trout family, a 97-pound, 4-ounce king salmon. Anderson's king salmon
(also known as a chinook), was landed from Alaska's Kenai River on
May 17, 1985. He played it for more than seven hours.   Photo: International
Sportsmen's Expositions

Figure 4.9.   Rainbow trout. World record: 42 pounds, 2 ounces, caught at Bell Island, Alaska, by David Robert White on June 22, 1970.
Photo: California Department of Fish and Game

Rainbow Trout

Rainbow trout (*Salmo gairdneri*) have been stocked in many lakes and reservoirs throughout the United States although they are native to the West, ranging from Alaska to Mexico, including Montana, Idaho, Nevada, Utah, and Colorado. Rainbows have several subspecies which differ in markings and coloration. Some spotted trouts have been cross-bred with rainbows.

Freshwater line-class records have come from such places as Rouge River, Michigan (18 pounds, 12 ounces); Pend Oreille Lake, Idaho (30 pounds, 9 ounces); Skeens River, Canada (29 pounds, 1 ounce); Lake Michigan, Illinois (16 pounds, 8 ounces); and Cowlitz River, Washington (18 pounds, 4 ounces).

Two fly rod world records for rainbows were set in Indiana, both by the same angler, Roger D. Enyeart. Those fish entered the books in September of 1981 and 1982 from Trail Creek and Little Calumet River. The top fly rod rainbow, 22 pounds, 8 ounces, was caught from Rogue River, Michigan.

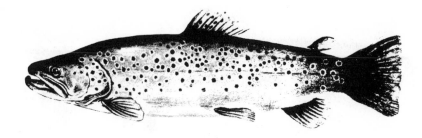

Figure 4.10. Brown trout. World record: 35 pounds, 15 ounces, caught at Nahuel Huapi, Argentina, by Eugenio Cavaglia on December 16, 1952. Photo: California Department of Fish and Game

Brown Trout

Brown trout (*Salmo trutta*), known also as German brown trout, were first transplanted from Europe to the United States. The first states to receive European brown trout were New York and Michigan in 1883 but soon after, the brown spread to many areas of north central and western United States.

Brown trout, like the Atlantic salmon, are speckled with black spots on their dark bronze bodies. Sometimes red spots with halos appear on their top sides near the head region; they are the only trout with both black and red spots.

World record browns have come from White River, Arkansas (33 pounds, 8 ounces and 27 pounds, 9 ounces) and Utah's Flaming Gorge Reservoir (33 pounds, 10 ounces). Joe Butler holds the top brown for all fly rod classes, a 27-pound, 3-ounce fish from Flaming Gorge Reservoir.

Fly patterns that brown trout anglers choose from include various larva and nymph imitations of their insect diets, particularly stoneflies, mayflies, and hellgrammite patterns. They are also enticed by spinners, spoons, and small minnow imitations, and will attack nightcrawlers, canned corn, salmon eggs, and marshmallows.

Similar to Atlantic salmon, sea-run brown trout migrate to fresh flowing streams to spawn. Browns that are strictly freshwater fish have adapted well, preferring cold mountain lakes and impoundments. They are a wary fish and often hard to catch; this explains why they dominate these lakes as aggressive predators of other trout and baitfishes.

Figure 4.11. Golden trout. World record: 11 pounds, caught in Cook's Lake, Wyoming, by Charles S. Reed on August 5, 1948. Photo: California Department of Fish and Game

Golden Trout

Golden trout (*Salmo aquabonita*), one of the smallest members of the trout family, is sought more for its beauty and challenge to backpackers as it is native only to Tulare and Kern Counties in California. It prefers cold Sierra lakes at elevations higher than 6,300 feet.

Its cheeks are red with white-tipped top and bottom fins. Its sides are bright shades of yellow and red, speckled above the lateral line with a few distinct black spots.

Figure 4.12. Brook trout. World record: 14 pounds, 8 ounces, caught in the Nipigon River, Canada, by Dr. W.J. Cook in July 1916. Photo: California Department of Fish and Game

Brook Trout

Eastern brook trout (*Salvelinus fontinalis*) prefer the cold streams and lakes in north central and northeastern United States and Canada. They exist in higher elevation lakes in West Coast mountain states but are native to the East. They have the ability to spawn in either fresh-running streams or springs in deep, natural lakes (*fontinalis* means "living in springs").

Sometimes brook trout go by the names speckled trout or mountain trout. They have squared rather than forked tails. Extreme warm water temperatures can kill brook trout; they inhabit cold streams that are usually 57 to 61 °F. A member of the *Salvelinus* group of trouts, brook trout are considered chars. Chars belong to the same family as trout but they are distinguished from other trouts by their lower fins, which have milk-white leading edges. Dark wavy lines rather than spots cover their backs. A series of red dots appear on their sides.

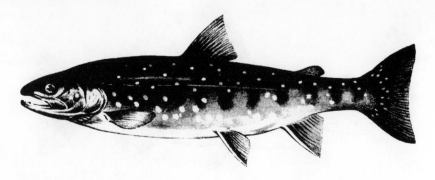

Figure 4.13. Dolly Varden. World record: 8 pounds, 1 ounce, caught in the Nakwasina River, Alaska, by Loyal J. Johnson on July 14, 1985.
Photo: California Department of Fish and Game

Dolly Varden

The name, Dolly Varden (*Salvelinus malma*), stems from a popular dress-making material which was worn by women members of a fishing party on the McCloud River in California in 1919. The pattern was unique because of its spots, a characteristic that also applies to the appearance of Dolly Varden, a char.

Dolly Varden primarily inhabit the Pacific Northwest states including Canada's British Columbia. They are close relatives of Arctic char and are anadromous fish that adapt readily to a landlocked environment.

Many salmon anglers consider the Dolly Varden a culprit because it likes to devour salmon eggs. Nevertheless it is a good tasting fish and provides plenty of action for fly rodders and spin casters alike.

It is often confused with bull trout of mountain lakes and with the Arctic char, which, except for differences in spot markings, is a mirror image of the Dolly. The spots on Dolly Varden are usually smaller than the pupils of their eyes. In contrast, the Arctic char has scattered pale yellow or pinkish-yellow spots that are larger than their pupils.

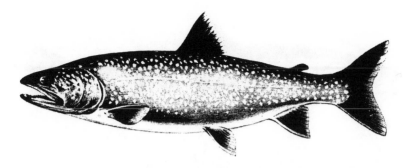

Figure 4.14. **Lake trout.** World record: 65 pounds, caught in Great Bear Lake, Canada, by Larry Daunis on August 8, 1970. Photo: California Department of Fish and Game

Lake Trout

Lake trout (*Salvelinus namaycush*) could, in all fairness, be called Great Bear Lake trout because that's where the biggest ones in the world are caught. They are chilly inhabitants of the Great Lakes and Canada, and have adapted well to being transplanted to cold western lakes. In a scientific sense, they are actually a char and are the largest nonmigratory trout-like fish.

They can't survive in saltwater. Instead, they prefer deep, cold lakes. One subspecies of lake trout has been caught 300 to 600 feet below the surface of Lake Superior.

At California's Lake Tahoe, which is one of the deepest lakes in the world, lake trout are caught by trolling deep plugs and spoons behind hundreds of feet of lead core line. In colder parts of the northern United States and throughout central Canada and the Northwest Territories, lake trout are considered to be the predatory champions of their environment; it is feared that they have the potential to wipe out populations of other freshwater trouts.

They are the only trout that don't cover their eggs with gravel. Instead, the hens drop their roe on shelves and ledges at the bottom of lakes.

Lake trout have more nicknames than the average fish. A few include Mackinaw, Great Lakes trout, laker, mountain trout, bank trout, and humper.

Lake trout were transplanted in 1894 from Michigan to California's Lake Tahoe, Donner Lake, and others in the Truckee River drainage. Its scientific name, *namaycush*, is an Indian name that dates back to 1792. They are dark gray to pale brown in color with pale white to dull orange spots. They have white-tipped fin borders, typical of a char.

Figure 4.15. Cutthroat trout. World record: 41 pounds, caught in
Pyramid Lake, Nevada, by John Skimmerhorn in December 1925.
Photo: California Department of Fish and Game

Cutthroat Trout

A cutthroat trout (*salmo clarki*) is a red-throated trout that gets its name
from the yellow or red streak beneath its lower jaw. The largest subspecies of cutthroat trout, the Lahontan cutthroat, once dominated California's Lake Tahoe, but was driven near extinction in the 1940s after
the transplantation of lake trout. During the 1920s, Lahontan trout from
the Truckee River averaged 20 pounds per fish. Other subspecies of
cutthroats are sea-run critters but freshwater cutthroats have flourished
in Rocky Mountain lakes.

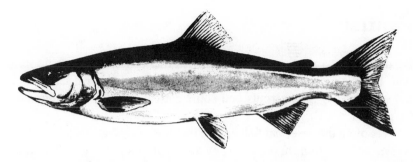

Figure 4.16.   Kokanee. World record: 6 pounds, 9 ounces, caught in Priest Lake, Idaho, by Jerry Verge on June 9, 1975.   Photo: California Department of Fish and Game

Kokanee

Kokanee (*Oncorhynchus nerka*) are a landlocked type of sockeye salmon. Its scientific name is Greek for "hooked nose of flowing waters." Although it is not a trout or a char, kokanee belong to the same family as trout.

They are blue with silver sides but turn deep red during spawning season. As in the case of sockeye salmon, male kokanees develop hooked lower jaws.

Panfish

By definition, a panfish is any small fish that can be fried whole in a pan. For the most part, panfish are members of the sunfish family but not necessarily. Small trouts and some catfish are also considered to be panfish.

As is often the case, panfish can be the most abundant fishes in Midwestern lakes and farm ponds. They are a curious group of fishes and, for that reason, provide unlimited action for the angler who is able to figure out what these fish are eating and entice them with something that arouses their curiosities.

One of the best aspects of angling for panfish is that once you've located them and are able to catch one, the second, third, and fourth fish usually strike with little hesitation. This consistent action and the simplicity of fishing for panfish on light tackle make this sport enjoyable.

Bluegill, redear sunfish, and crappie (pronounced, "krop•ee") are typical panfish which have small mouths. Anglers who have trouble catching panfish after they strike should consider using smaller hooks. All of these fish are fascinated by lead-headed mini-jigs or doll flies. The red-on-white color combination is a standby for crappies although patterns will vary with water clarity and the characteristics of their particular habitat.

A smart panfisher will experiment with fishing at different depths to find the depth at which the fish are suspended. Wind direction and plankton flow should weigh in your consideration for locating these feisty fighters. Look for them near fallen trees and submerged bushes, or around rock ledges in deep reservoirs.

They are a sport fish that merit the use of ultra-light gear. A cane pole with a bobber will suffice for angling tools, but a game fisher who plans to make this a regular sport should go at them with a small spin caster, levelwind, or spinning reel. Don't forget to use small hooks.

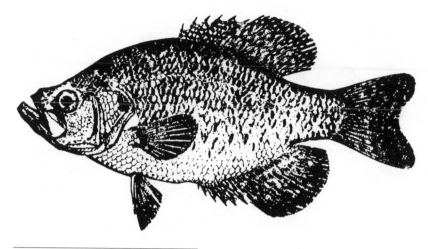

Figure 4.17. White crappie. World record: 5 pounds, 3 ounces, caught
at Enid Dam, Mississippi, by Fred L. Bright on July 31, 1957.
Photo: California Department Fish and Game

Crappie

There are two types of crappies that dominate the United States where
they are native to the East. Black crappies (*Pomoxis nigromaculatus*)
have adapted well to sluggish waters of the South. White crappie
(*Pomoxis annularis*) don't have the distinct dark markings as black
crappie but prefer the same type of watershed.

A relatively short-lived fish, adult crappie spawn in large groups near
banks and bushy underwater structures. This happens between May and
June when water temperature is 62 to 68 °F. They seldom exceed
5 years of age.

Unlike most other sunfishes, crappies continue feeding throughout
mild winters, which is a good time to fish for them. They are minnow
eaters and reproduce rapidly, something that fish management specialists
keep track of so that crappie don't overpopulate a lake and stunt the
size of the average fish.

Aside from obvious darker markings of black crappie as compared
to the lighter tones of silver-colored white crappie, a distinguishing
characteristic of the two is the number of dorsal spines. Black crappies
have seven to eight dorsal spines. White crappie have only six.

Figure 4.18.   Black crappie. World record: 4 pounds, 8 ounces, caught in Kerr Lake, Virginia, by L. Carl Herring on March 1, 1981.   Photo: California Department Fish and Game

Pomoxis means "sharp gill cover," descriptive of the shape of its gill plate, which is unlike the round ear flap design of most sunfishes. Crappie also have larger mouths than most sunfish but not nearly the size of their cousins, the largemouth and smallmouth bass.

Crappie will attack most small, live minnows that are dangled in range of their extensive peripheral vision. Larger crappies are known to strike small, jointed minnow-imitation lures, the kind that are normally used for black bass fishing. A spinner, sometimes, is irresistible to them.

Figure 4.19. Bluegill. World record: 4 pounds, 12 ounces, caught in Ketona Lake, Alabama, by T.S. Hudson on April 9, 1950. Photo: California Department of Fish and Game

Bluegill

Bluegill (*Lepomis macrochirus*) have the appearance of slab-like sunfish. They are distinguished by their copper-colored bellies and their black, rounded gill cover flaps.

Also called bream and slabbies, these colorful sunfish exist throughout the United States, but they are native to the East. Bluegill are fond of crickets, red worms, and pieces of night crawlers. Mini-jigs and small lures also attract them.

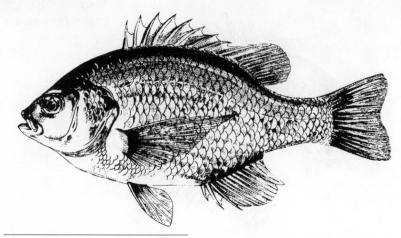

Figure 4.20. Redear sunfish. World record: 4 pounds, 13 ounces, caught in Merritt's Mill Pond, Florida, by Joey M. Floyd on March 13, 1986. Photo: California Department of Fish and Game

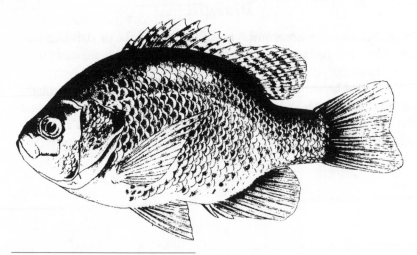

Figure 4.21. Pumpkinseed. No world record is listed. Photo: California Department of Fish and Game

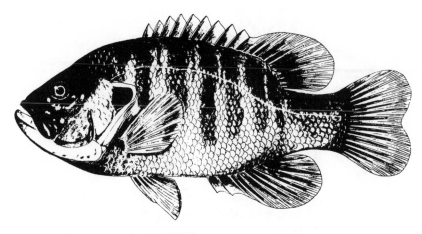

Figure 4.22. Green sunfish. World record: 2 pounds, 2 ounces, caught in Stockton Lake, Missouri, by Paul M. Dilley on June 18, 1971.
Photo: California Department of Fish and Game

Redear Sunfish

The redear sunfish (*Lepomis microlophus*) looks similar to its close relative, the pumpkinseed (*Lepomis gibbosus*). The two are distinguished by the flexibility of their gill flaps. The gill cover of a redear sunfish can be bent at right angles while a pumpkinseed's is more rigid.

Redears are bigger than the average bluegill. They prefer deep, quiet ponds and sloughs. They spawn more than once per year as water temperatures approach 75 °F. For the most part they are bottom feeders, thriving on small clams and snails.

Green Sunfish

Green sunfish (*Lepomis cyanellus*) adapt easily to new habitats although they are most often found in the same type of environment as bluegills. Biologists have found that green sunfish have a high tolerance for warm water temperature. Some are able to withstand water that is 97 °F. They thrive on small aquatic insects and minnows.

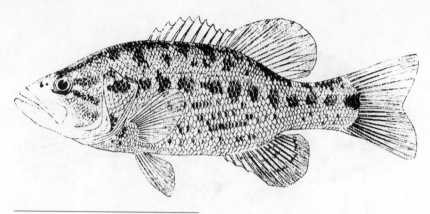

Figure 4.23. Spotted bass. World record: 8 pounds, 15 ounces, caught in Lewis Smith Lake, Alabama, by Philip C. Terry, Jr. on March 18, 1978. Photo: California Department of Fish and Game

Spotted Bass

Spotted bass (*Micropterus punctulatus*) resembles its black bass cousins, the smallmouth and largemouth. However, its first and second dorsal fins are connected and it doesn't have the vertical bars, which are typical of a smallmouth bass. Instead, it has small black spots below its lateral line. There are three subspecies of the spotted bass including the northern spotted bass, the Alabama spotted bass, and the Wichita spotted bass.

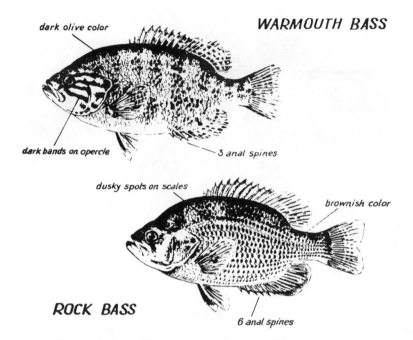

dark olive color

WARMOUTH BASS

dark bands on opercle

3 anal spines

dusky spots on scales

brownish color

ROCK BASS

6 anal spines

Figure 4.24. Rock bass. World record: 3 pounds, caught in York River, Canada, by Peter Gulgin on August 1, 1974. **Warmouth bass.** World record: 2 pounds, 2 ounces, caught at Douglas Swamp, South Carolina, by Willie Singletary on March 19, 1973. Photo: Wisconsin Fisheries Management Department

Rock Bass/Warmouth Bass

Rock bass (*Ambloplites rupestris*) and warmouth bass (*Lepomis gulosus*) are two sunfishes that look like a cross between a bluegill and a black bass. Primarily northern game fishes, they have been found as far south as Alabama and have been transplanted to some western states.

The rock bass prefers cool, weedy rivers, streams, and reservoirs and likes to hang out over rocky bottoms as its name implies.

The warmouth, a pond fish, differs from the rock bass in that it has three anal spines as compared to six on the rock bass. It also has more distinct markings including a dark olive coloration along its back and dark bands on its gill plate.

Figure 4.25.   Yellow perch. World record: 4 pounds, 3 ounces, caught in Bordentown, New Jersey, by Dr. C.C. Abbot in May 1865.   Photo: California Department of Fish and Game

Yellow Perch

Yellow perch (*Perca flavescens*) provide northern anglers with year-round action even in ice-covered lakes. Distinctly yellow with six dark, vertical bands lining their sides, yellow perch are close relatives of walleye and sauger. They are not a bass as is the white perch (*Morone americana*).

Popular in Great Lakes states and extending to upper reaches of Canada's Northwest Territories, they are often devoured by larger northern game fishes, particularly pike and muskie.

Top perch waters in the nation include Saint Mary's River in Sault Sainte Marie, Michigan; Wordens Pond at South Kingston, Rhode Island; and lakes around Williamsburg, Virginia.

Catfish

The family of catfishes (*Ictaluridae*) is different from all other fish groups because all native American catfishes have scaleless bodies. You'll know when you catch a catfish if it has, rather than scales, a smooth, slimy skin and long barbels dangling from the corners of its mouth.

Catfish go by the nicknames whisker jaws, cats, flatheads, bullheads, and fiddlers. They are bottom feeders with a keen sense of smell which makes it easy for them to detect the foul scent of what's known as stink baits: chicken livers, cheeses, and dough balls.

Catfish are raised commercially for their fast growth and food value. They are a prize for the skillet and a challenge for anglers in every part of the nation.

As a river fish, catfish lay low in holes of meandering Midwestern rivers. They feed in stiff currents like slimy submarines plotting an attack. Once at war, they are merciless fighters, having injured many an angler, who had battled them to the shore but forgot about their sharp dorsal and pectoral spines. Catfish make for a dangerous fencing partner, a thought to consider when landing one.

They are hardy, prehistoric-looking critters with beady eyes and long whiskers and mouths made for swallowing silvery baitfish sideways. Like most other fishes, they attack their victims head first with a powerful pinch from two brush-toothed lips.

Their skin is tough; some catfish can live for minutes to more than an hour out of water depending on the temperature and humidity. They live long lives by evidence of the largest blue catfish: a hulking 97-pounder taken from the Missouri River in South Dakota in 1959.

An occasional catfish is caught on artificial bait, usually spinners or rubber-tailed jigs. Virtually any raw meat, especially chicken livers and dead fish, will entice catfish. Live baits such as nightcrawlers, large minnows, and catalpa worms appeal to some of the biggest catfish.

Unlike most other freshwater fishes, a catfish has the unique ability to generate sound by sending vibrations from its swim bladder through a series of tiny bones that are similar to those of a human's ear. This grunting sound, a throaty purr, can sometimes be heard after a catfish has been hooked and landed.

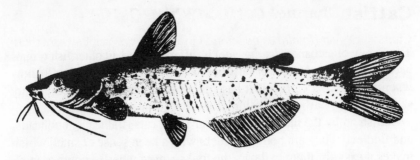

Figure 4.26.   Channel catfish. World record: 58 pounds, caught in the Santee-Cooper Reservoir, South Carolina, by W.B. Whaley on July 7, 1964. Photo: California Department of Fish and Game

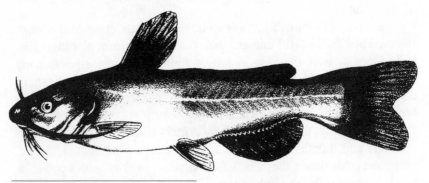

Figure 4.27.   White catfish. World record: 17 pounds, 7 ounces, caught in Success Lake, California, by Chuck Idell on November 15, 1981. Photo: California Department of Fish and Game

Figure 4.28.   Blue catfish. World record: 97 pounds, caught in the Missouri River, South Dakota, by Edward B. Elliott on September 16, 1959. Photo: California Department of Fish and Game

Channel Catfish/White Catfish

Channel catfish (*Ictalurus punctatus*) look different from all other catfish because of their deep-forked tails and irregular spots that dot their bodies. Sometimes this bluish or brown/blue fish is confused with white catfish (*Ictalurus catus*), which also is bluish to grayish in color and has a deep-forked tail. One difference between the two is the number of rays in the anal fin. A channel catfish has 24 to 29 rays, while a white catfish has only 19 to 23 rays in its rear, underside fin.

Channel catfish tend to prefer clean environments: swift rivers, large lakes, and waterways with sand or gravel bottoms.

Blue Catfish

Blue catfish (*Ictalurus furcatus*) is the only other type of catfish that has a forked tail. It differs from channel and white catfish in that it has 30 to 36 rays in its anal fin.

Blues have lived for centuries in the Mississippi, Missouri, and Ohio river systems. There may be truth behind stories told by divers who were sent to inspect the bottoms of large dams at reservoirs; some have reported catfish in excess of 120 pounds.

Figure 4.29. Flathead catfish. World record: 91 pounds, 4 ounces, in Lake Lewisville, Texas, by Mike Rogers on March 28, 1982.   Photo: California Department of Fish and Game

Flathead Catfish

Flathead catfish (*Pylodictis olivaris*) may be another cause of fear to skin divers who probe deep lakes and reservoirs in the midwestern and southern United States. Flatheads have been known to exceed 90 pounds and most are probably larger than some anglers who stalk them.

Flatheads are generally dark brown with olive and yellow patterns on their upper backs and upper sides. They are active during the night, consuming crayfish, worms, and baitfish. They spawn during June and, like other catfishes, they nest in undercut river banks or against logs and submerged objects. Flatheads weighing more than 20 pounds are not uncommon.

Bullhead Catfish

There are three smaller catfish that inhabit ponds, lakes, and streams in the United States. They are called bullheads for their mean-looking appearance.

The brown bullhead (*Ictalurus nebulosus*) is typical of the others, which are identified by their color, namely the black (*melas*) and yellow (*natalis*) species.

Yellow bullhead catfish, often called yellow bellies, inhabit lakes, ponds, and shallow streams. They thrive on insects and small fishes. Like their two cousins, they'd probably eat a crawdad if you offered one to them.

The bullheads all have squared tails, which is an easy way to distinguish them from young channel catfish. Bullheads spawn at 70 °F but can live in waters as cold as 32 °F and as warm as 98 °F. They adapt to very low oxygen levels, which explains why they are one of the hardiest fish on this planet.

Figure 4.30. Brown bullhead. World record: 5 pounds, 8 ounces, caught in Veal Pond, Georgia, by Jimmy Andrews on May 22, 1975.
Photo: California Department of Fish and Game

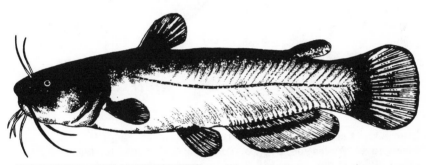

Figure 4.31. Yellow bullhead. World record: 4 pounds, 4 ounces, caught in Mormon Lake, Arizona, by Emily Williams on May 11, 1984.
Photo: California Department of Fish and Game

Figure 4.32. Black bullhead. World record: 8 pounds, caught in Lake Waccabuc, New York, by Kani Evans on August 1, 1951. Photo: California Department of Fish and Game

Carp

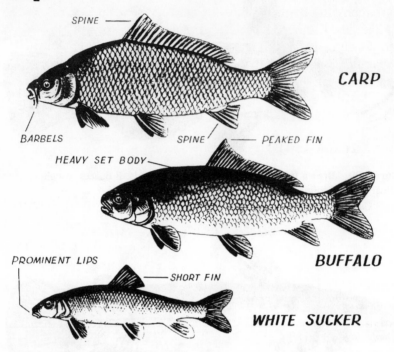

SPINE

CARP

BARBELS   SPINE   PEAKED FIN

HEAVY SET BODY

BUFFALO

PROMINENT LIPS

SHORT FIN

WHITE SUCKER

Figure 4.33. Carp. World record: 57 pounds, 13 ounces, caught in Potomac River, Washington, D.C., by David Nikolow on June 19, 1983. **Buffalo.** World record: 70 pounds, 5 ounces, caught at Bussey Brake, Louisiana, by Delbert Sisk on April 21, 1980. **White sucker.** Close relative of the carp. Photo: Wisconsin Fisheries Management Department

Carp (*Cyprinus carpio*), bigmouth buffalo (*Ictiobus cyprinellus*), and the white sucker are large-scaled fishes that seem to survive where most other fishes don't. They are considered to be rough fishes as opposed to a prized game fish but they grow to large sizes and often are bigger than most fishes in their habitats.

They don't take readily to most baits offered on hook-and-line. They do, however, "sucker" for dough balls and worms. A few ardent fly fishermen have successfully tempted them with fly patterns.

Carp and buffalo fish can be seen rising to the surface of warm, midwestern and northern lakes during summer months. They have sent chills through the spine of more than one bass fisherman who thought that what he or she had witnessed was a school of world-class bass.

When carp or buffalo roll at the surface, they can be distinguished from trophy fish by their yellowish flash. A close-up look will reveal red-like fins. Carp and buffalo are regular catches of trot lines baited with dough balls.

Suckers, so named because of the shape of their lips, make for excellent baitfish in northern lakes and rivers.

Northern Game Fish

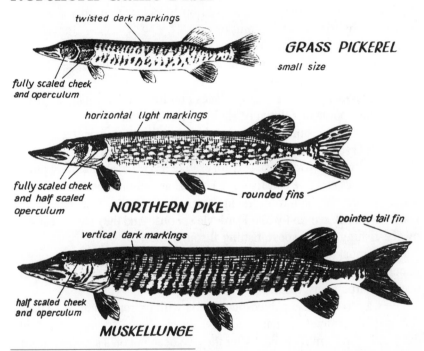

Figure 4.34. **Grass pickerel.** World record: 9 pounds, 6 ounces, caught in Homerville, Georgia, by Baxley McQuaig, Jr. on February 17, 1961. **Northern pike.** World record: 46 pounds, 2 ounces, caught in the Sacandaga Reservoir, New York, by Peter Dubuc on September 15, 1940. **Muskellunge.** World record: 69 pounds, 15 ounces, caught in the St. Lawrence River, New York, by Arthur Lawton on September 22, 1957. Photo: Wisconsin Fisheries Management Department

Muskies and Northern Pike

There is an old saying for anglers in Wisconsin, Minnesota, Michigan, Ohio, Pennsylvania, and upstate New York which goes something like this: "The average fisherman catches only one muskie in his lifetime if he's able to even hook one." Catching a mighty muskellunge, therefore, must be one of the most challenging aspects of freshwater fishing.

Muskellunge (*Esox masquinongy*) and its relative, the tiger muskie (*Esox masquinongy x Esox lucius*) are the superior varieties of northern game fish. They are bigger on the average than their cousins, the northern pike (*Esox lucius*) and the pickerel (*Esox niger*). But, the northeast and north central United States and nearly all of Canada and inland Alaska offer some opportunities for catching 25- and 30-pound pike.

It was once thought that there were four species of muskellunge, but the International Game Fish Association has classified only one (except for a hybrid, the tiger muskie).

Leech Lake, Minnesota is famous for producing large muskies as are 1,000 Island Lake, Michigan; Lake of the Woods on the U.S.-Canada border; and the Wisconsin River.

The muskie seeks dark hiding places and likes to hunt its prey from the vantage point of relatively shallow weed beds.

Unlike muskies, northern pike can be taken with some degree of success on fly rods, particularly on the McKenzie River and in Great Slave Lake in Canada's Northwest Territory. Pike are usually caught by plugging, trolling, and live bait fishing. Their sharp teeth often require wire leaders to prevent them from fraying monofilament line. They have been known to attack red-and-white Dardevle spoons. And they can be caught by ice fishing or by spear fishing through the ice.

Pikes, muskies, and the more bass-like walleyes differ from other fishes by their scaled, elongated bodies, their pointed noses, and their needle-sharp, spiny teeth.

The way to handle a played-out pike is with extreme caution. These fish are determined animals and have been known to snap at a lure dangled behind a moving boat after they've been put on a stringer. Their diet is nothing short of ducklings, mice, and oversized live minnows. In case you get stuck in the unfortunate dilemma of having to land a northern pike or muskie without a net or gaff, take caution to subdue the fish by pinching its eye sockets together or else you'll injure a finger that will be slow to heal.

Pike and muskies have long, broad, flat mouths that are similar to the bill of a duck. They are generally green shades of greenish-gray color with pale white or yellow markings. Their cousins, the walleyes, are somewhat of a walleyed pike-perch and, as such, are often called that.

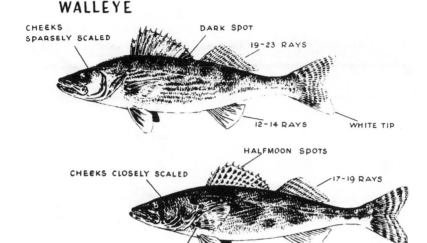

Figure 4.35. Walleye. World record: 25 pounds, caught in Old Hickory Lake, Tennessee, by Mabry Harper on August 1, 1960. **Sauger.** World record: 8 pounds, 12 ounces, caught in Lake Sakakawea, North Dakota, by Mike Fischer on October 6, 1971.   Photo: Wisconsin Fisheries Management Department

Walleye/Sauger

The walleye (*Stizostedion vitreum vitreum*) inhabits basically the same places as northerns and muskies. It is actually a member of the perch grouping but much larger than a perch with some exceeding 20 pounds.

A walleye's first cousin, the sauger (*Stizostedion canadense*) is almost identical to the walleye in appearance. The difference is a dark blotch, which can be found at the base of a walleye's first dorsal fins. Saugers have a series of spots on both dorsal fins with no blotch.

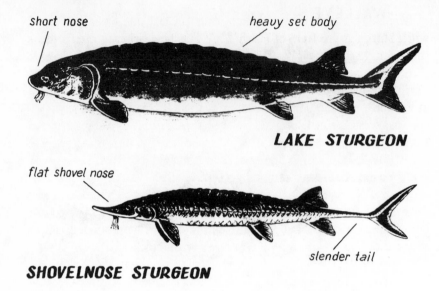

short nose

heavy set body

LAKE STURGEON

flat shovel nose

slender tail

SHOVELNOSE STURGEON

Figure 4.36. Sturgeon. World record: 468 pounds, caught at Benicia, California, by Joey Pallotta on July 9, 1983. Photo: Wisconsin Fisheries Management Department

Sturgeon

White sturgeon (*Acipenseridae transmontanus*), the largest North American game fish, have mystified anglers for centuries. They are prehistoric-looking creatures with long bodies and pointed, barbeled snouts.

Their white-meated torso is protected by tough skin and rows of razor-sharp, diamond-shaped plates which give them an armor-like appearance. They have soft mouths protected by hard plates. A fleshy hose dangles from the snout's bottomside. It channels food to the fish as it pecks along the bottom of bays, rivers, and lakes like a giant chicken on the feed. In many ways a sturgeon's mouth resembles a vacuum cleaner hose and provides much the same function: to suck up things.

Sturgeon have small eyes as compared to the size of their bodies. They feed primarily by smell as they probe the bottoms. They are anadromous fish which journey to fresher water to spawn.

There are seven species of sturgeon in North America. Sixteen exist throughout the world with some of the biggest found in the Soviet Union. Their black, sticky roe is considered a delicacy and their meat is appealing and often underrated although it is clean and white.

Sturgeon eat all kinds of shrimp, crustaceans, and baitfish. Pacific white sturgeon are fond of herring roe but their primary diet is grass shrimp, mud shrimp, ghost shrimp, and clams. They range from Canada to Florida on the East Coast and from British Columbia to California along the West Coast. Some of the largest have been caught and released in Washington's Columbia River and Idaho's Snake River. At least two species of landlocked sturgeon, lake and shovelnose, inhabit lakes and streams in the Great Lakes area. The shovelnose variety is found in the Missouri and Mississippi rivers and their tributaries.

It's no wonder that sturgeon are often called "tackle busters" because of their unusual fighting abilities. When hooked, they will roll their armor-like bodies in the line, trying to shear it on their sharp edges. For this reason sturgeon stalkers use plastic-coated, wire-braided leaders above their hooks or some type of heavy monofilament.

Sometimes sturgeon can be seen jumping or rising rapidly toward the surface. Sportsmen who have fished for them say this is how sturgeons clean mud from their gill rakers.

Joey Pallotta of Crockett, California, set the freshwater record for a sturgeon in 1983. After battling it for five hours in the Carquinez Straights between San Francisco's San Pablo and Suisun bays, he managed to land the beast on 80-pound test line. It weighed 468 pounds and measured 9 feet, 6 inches. Biologists estimated that it was 100 years old.

Many sturgeon along the Pacific Coast have tipped the scales at 100 and 200 pounds. A program supported by the United Anglers of California to stock the Sacramento River with sturgeon that were raised in captivity at the University of California at Davis, has greatly enhanced the numbers of smaller sturgeon during the 1980s.

Figure 5.1. (opposite page) Ron Sittinger, the man behind the toothpick trick, is a versatile angler by evidence of these American shad that he caught using self-tied shad flies and his custom-made fly rod.
Photo: Keith Rogers

chapter
5

Tackle

Yip Yungner snapped down the straps on his hip waders and prepared for the march through Mallard Slough. We had left his home at 7 o'clock that frosty November morning, vowing to navigate the unfamiliar marshland during the daylight hours. Our destination was a point on the tule-flocked shoreline of Suisun Bay, a three-mile walk in mud up to our knees where rabbit trails were the only firm ground. Not a tree stood in the forest before us. Instead there was a maze of reed-like weeds, taller than our eyes could see. It was a place at the mouth of the slough where big diamondback sturgeon wrestled 50-foot currents within casting range from the shore. In that part of the marsh, these monstrous, prehistoric fish with diamond-shaped scales on their backs were often referred to as slugs.

Yip stood on the dirt road where we had locked the car. He was wearing jersey number 11 from the Gold Street Jets. On his head was a red, white, and blue baseball cap emblazoned with the words, "Boondocks U.S.A." These, he said, were his luckiest articles of clothing. And though he never said he was superstitious, it seems that every time we went fishing, Yip wore the jersey from his hockey team in Minnesota and a hat from a place in Iowa where he had always had good luck pheasant hunting.

Having come from the Midwest, he was not accustomed to fishing for sturgeon, the largest North American freshwater game fish, nor was he ready to tackle the problem with the right tools. He hauled a trout rod in one hand. Mounted on it was a spinning reel which had a small-capacity spool loaded with 4-pound monofilament test line. It was light-weight equipment for a heavyweight job.

He locked the car door before grabbing the cooler with our lunch in it, then took his first sticky step into the marsh. We carried a map that I had traced from a Coast Guard navigational chart. It showed every waterway, the most visible landmarks, the water depths, and a few roads. It told us little about the thickets and the hummocks along the way.

Hungry for sturgeon, we thrashed through the mucky, lily-pad jungle carrying with us the necessary gear: fishing rods, live bait on ice, a bucket of live bullheads, one green, long-handled net, and our rain-coats. We took my tackle box and left Yip's in the car. We each had stuffed a couple of 8-ounce lead sinkers in our pockets, figuring that's what it would take to hold our shrimp in the current.

"Think we got it all," Yip had mumbled as a bead of sweat trickled from his curly, blond beard and dampened the neckline of his jersey.

I said nothing but stopped for a second to watch a jackrabbit cross our trail. Then we shed our jackets and continued plodding through the bog, searching for a low spot to ford a slough so that we could hike the rest of the way to the point by the sturgeon hole.

Having found no such spot, we elected to fish the slough while we examined the "treasure hunt" map that would take us to where we thought the slugs were feeding.

At low tide, I discovered a wooden platform floating off a post on the opposite bank. It was only a short swim, and though it was November, I felt it was worth a brief dip in the chilly water to get our tackle to the other side and have a solid place from which to fish. I only had to swim as far as it was wide and then another 15 yards. I quickly shed everything but my gym shorts and slid quietly into the slough. While breast-stroking the entire way, I paused occasionally to touch bottom with one foot. I discovered it was over my head in only one spot. When I reached the platform to pull myself out of the water, I noticed a portion of one plywood section was covered with bird droppings. Obviously, it had been a perch for many gulls, an indication they had feasted not far from the platform.

I tied a short rope using a metal fence stake which we had found on the shore. We used it for the rest of the voyage as a pole to maneuver the platform by poking along the bottom. I had to get in the water once more to push the platform around the last knob of tules that stood between us and the bay.

Because it was low tide, we anchored by staking the platform at the high water line. I dried off while Yip baited the hooks; then we each lobbed a line about 30 yards out.

Two hours passed before the tide turned around. Neither of us had gotten a nibble. In fact, the action was so slow that Yip had dozed off and was sleeping soundly when a barge heading up river sent out a wake that nearly washed us off the platform. I roused him seconds before the wave slammed into us. He grabbed the rods while I scrambled for the net. We both reached for the cooler just as it was about to slide overboard.

"Holy cow," Yip gasped, wide-eyed and a bit wet. "We were lucky."

His last words proved to be the understatement of the day as no sooner had he finished saying "lucky" when the tip of his trout rod nodded three times in succession. Immediately he laid the larger rod on the deck and yanked back on the smaller rod.

Instantly it doubled over and Yip bellowed, "Fish on! She's comin' your way."

Like a flash of light, it ran his 4-pound monofilament nearly down to a bare spool before the fish changed directions and headed back for the platform. He reeled quickly trying to catch up with it. When he reached that point, his line went from slack to taut. His fiberglass rod froze in an arched position, pointing straight downward.

"Yahoo," Yip shouted. "She's still on there."

I readied the net by popping out its extender handle and locking it in place. All the commotion had caught the attention of several boats passing by which dropped anchor outside of the battle zone. They were the audience and we were the actors on a floating stage. Yip's fish wouldn't budge. For another five minutes it hung in the hole, shaking its head and occasionally setting Yip's drag, "zing, zing, zing." Suddenly the fish began to move and Yip's line came up and up and up. He reeled furiously, trying once again to catch up with it.

Out of the corner of my eye, I noticed the other spinning rod swing across the deck. With the net in one hand, I grabbed the rod with the other and levied a quick, punchy jerk; then laid it back on the deck and stepped on its cork handle with the heel of my hip wader to keep it from getting pulled into the river.

Now we had two fish hooked up and Yip had worked his within a few yards of the platform. It rolled once near the surface, showing its long gray and white body. There was no doubt about it, he had hooked into a nice sturgeon, about 5 feet.

The second time Yip's fish rolled, it was within netting range of the platform but obviously was not tired out. It ducked under the platform just as I was about to make a stab at it with the net and then it headed back for the bay. In doing this, it had wedged Yip's line between a plank and a rusty nail on the underside of the platform. The line snapped instantly, and Yip threw his hands up in disgust.

Seeing that disappointment was about to overwhelm him, I dropped the net and plucked the other rod from under my foot.

"Here," I said, handing it to him. "Play this one."

He raised one eyebrow but accepted the offer. He even cracked a smile when he felt the fish tugging at the end of the line. It was a much smaller sturgeon than the one with which he had just battled. It was already played out to some extent after having set the drag off and on during the past five minutes. He worked that one to the platform with no problem and I swooped it up in the big green net. We slapped each other a "high five" while the audience of boaters cheered and waved.

The sturgeon turned out to be 39 inches, an inch short of the minimum keeper length, so we released it and continued to fish for another hour with no strikes. One boater who anchored in the hole caught another shaker and released it. Yip had a feeling the boat's unsportsmanlike action of anchoring where we had found the fish might have had something to do with our sudden change of luck.

It was a chilly swim back to our portage at the slough. We anchored the dilapidated dock where we had found it, dried off with our T-shirts and put on our hip waders. Dog-tired and punchless from battling the slugs, we lugged our gear back through the muck. "At least we played one," I told Yip.

He muttered something about the guy in the boat; that's all that was said until we reached the car. That's where the agony of the day's fruitless venture set in. While we were gone, someone broke into my car and took Yip's tackle box and three red Frisbees which were in the back seat.

Rods and Reels

When Yip and I went shopping for new gear we searched for equipment designed for the fish we were trying to catch. We learned that a fisherman doesn't use an ultralight trout rod to tackle something the size of a sturgeon. The reverse holds true for trout. Trying to toss a spinner for trout with 30-pound test line and a conventional reel the size of a coffee can won't work either.

Scientific advances in materials fabrication during the 1960s and 1970s revolutionized the tackle sales industry. Rods and reels are made of more stress-resistant materials that enable anglers to take on heavy-weight tasks with lighter equipment than in the days of rods made from cane and reels made from hard rubber and nickel. Today's rods and reels are made of stuff that's stronger, longer lasting, friction-proof, and, more often than not, synthetic. Some reels employ the use of ball bearings and magnet systems that make it easier for a bait caster to toss lures and rigs with less chance for backlash. Ball bearings and synthetic, self-lubricating materials let anglers play fish with smooth instead of jerky pressure on the line. The best reels have parts made of alloys: graphite and metals that are rustproof and salt-resistant.

Even the high-technology angler must match the gear for the task. Anglers today can choose from rods made of fiberglass, boron, and graphite, or combinations of the three. Selecting the most appropriate material depends on the individual who will be using it.

In any case, the rod and a reel should be a balanced pair. Anglers trying to heave heavy line on a big reel with a short, lightweight rod will find the task less difficult when a smaller reel and lighter line are used.

Rods come in three classes, each named for the type of reel that they are designed for: spinning rods, bait casting rods, and fly rods.

Spinning Rods

Spinning rods consist of a fiberglass, boron, or graphite stick mounted on a long handle made of cork or reinforced synthetic sponge material. This butt section of the rod is sometimes hollow, as is the shaft. The reel seat, where the reel is fitted, is aligned with a series of eyelets secured to the shaft by wrappings of thread. The eyelets decrease in size as they descend toward the rod tip at which point a cap eyelet is placed.

Professional anglers make their own rods or have them custom-made to fit their preference for casting. Wrapping rods in secure and attractive thread patterns is an art of its own. Pro rod builders often recommend stainless steel eyelets lined with graphite, ceramic, or some type of friction-resistant material. These materials not only have less resistance to a line sliding through them, but also generally don't become scratched or nicked as easily with use, thus reducing the chance of putting fray in the line.

Spinning rods come in single, double, or multisectional pieces that can be broken down for easy portability. The length of the rod should correspond to the caster's ability and the task for which it is designed. If you plan to do a lot of long-distance plugging in a lake for pike or striped bass, a long rod (8 to 9 feet) with a lot of backbone for tossing large plugs inside the imaginary 50-yard line is required. This same rod, however, might prove cumbersome for trying to cast from a shoreline that's loaded with overhung branches and dense brush. Chances are you'll be fishing for largemouth bass, walleye, trout, or panfish in these conditions, in which cases you'll need a smaller flipping stick, one that requires one hand to toss it with the flick of the wrist. This is an ideal setup for hitting the mark around logs and brush piles.

In the hands of an angler who's rehearsed his or her casting, a spinning rod is a valuable tool that is hard to beat in almost any condition. It's a good starting point for the person who wants to learn fishing.

Bait Casting Rods

Bait casting rods are designed exactly for what their name implies: casting bait. For years they have provided an adequate function in plugging and lobbing artificial baits in both fresh and salt water conditions. Today, it is rare to find a professional black bass fisherman without a graphite or boron ultralight bait casting rod mounted with a small level-wind reel.

Once mastered, the bait casting rod and reel setup provides a versatile fishing tool with the advantage of a smooth, star-type drag for playing fish. Bait casting rods can be used to lob a bait, flip a plastic worm, sidearm a spinner, or toss a minijig underhanded. They are perhaps the best all-around rod for playing fish and are usually shorter and stouter than spinning rods. Ultralights, as opposed to medium- and heavy-action rods, provide better action in the rod tip for working plastic worms. Medium- and lightweight bait casting rods with their pistol grip butt sections appear similar to rods designed for closed-face, push-button type reels.

Fly Rods

Fly rods, like spinning rods, generally come in matched sections, some that can be broken down in many pieces so that even a long rod can be packed in to a remote lake or stream. These rods too are made of synthetic materials although some of the most expensive are made of bamboo cane or a limber but sturdy wood. Cane rods in this era of fishing are often regarded as collector's items.

Fly rods have line guides made of the same, innovative materials as eyelets of spinning rods. Guides as opposed to eyelets let a fly line slide with more freedom along the rod, an essential element for proper casting. Fly rods are designed differently from spinning rods in that the reel seat is positioned at the end of the cork or synthetic sponge handle instead of in the middle of the grip for better balance in casting and operation of the fly reel. Some fly rods do, however, come equipped with a ''fighting butt'' that can be attached to the end of the rod to give an angler more leverage in playing big fish.

Fly reels, like all fishing reels, should be loaded with a certain amount of backing, a type of braided dacron or similar material which is tied to the spool of the reel to prevent powerful fish from running out line so fast that it crushes the spool from acceleration and centrifugal force. Monofilament line, which can roll off a spool rapidly, is then tied to the slower moving backing.

Fly reels consist of a frame that has a pillar or crosspiece below which the line exits the spool. The spool is configured into a head plate, spool cap, and short, stout handle that fits inside the frame. The frame is also fashioned with a foot that fits into the reel seat. Standard fly reels don't have a lot of gears, bearings, or springs typical of spinning and bait-casting reels. The exception is the antireverse fly reel which does have a drag system. More advanced antireverse fly reels come with self-lubricating washers and slip rings.

Always take care of rods and reels. Movable parts on reels should be oiled as recommended by the manufacturer. When you have finished fishing, wipe moisture from rods and transport them in a tough case to prevent breakage.

The Toothpick Trick

The "toothpick trick" should be a verse in any bait fisherman's bible. Every September my fishing buddies thought I was crazy when I showed up at the docks with a toothpick lashed to the fat part of my spinning rod. Toothpicks and rubber bands are perhaps the least expensive items in an angler's tackle box, but they are priceless when it comes to eliminating line tension on the average spinning rod. Line tension is what fish feel when they pick up a baited hook attached to a line. Line tension causes pike, striped bass, and channel catfish to drop a bait that they normally would swallow. To eliminate it, all you need is a toothpick and a pair of rubber bands.

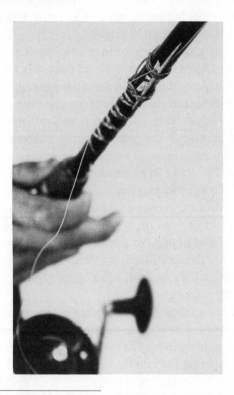

Figure 5.2.   Line wedged between a toothpick and the thick part of a spinning rod eliminates line tension when fishing with bait. Photo: Michael Macor

I heard about the toothpick trick when I fished the vanguard of the fall striped bass run in Honker Bay, 30 miles inland of San Francisco at the mouth of California's longest river, the Sacramento. This spot is not far from where striped bass were transplanted in West Coast waters.

According to what I know, a former San Francisco Bay deckhand, Ron Sittinger, invented the toothpick trick in the 1960s. The theory behind it has been used in one form or another since anglers first started fishing for stripers on the West Coast at the turn of the century. Chinese immigrants practiced the same method by piling line on the floor of their boats, holding it in place with a heavy coin or a can filled with a little water. When a fish would attack the bait, it would pop the line from underneath the coin, causing it to ping. Or the can would tip over as the fish tried to swim away with the line piled on the deck. This way, the fishermen could tell when a fish was on the line without keeping the line too tense.

When I fished with Sittinger, we'd use a piece of black electrical tape to secure a round toothpick on the underside of a spinning rod. It acted as a clip to hold line. Later, I modified this setup using a pair of rubber bands instead of the tape. Rubber bands don't come unglued in the rain and they add a spring-loaded effect to this makeshift clip.

The mechanics behind the toothpick trick are simple. With a spinning rod and reel, cast out a baited hook. Let it settle to the bottom but don't turn the reel's crank handle. Allow the wire-like bale on the reel to remain open. Then, carefully take the line and wedge it between the clip formed by the toothpick and rubber bands. This will hold your line in place so that you don't have to hold it for hours between your thumb and forefinger to wait for a fish to bite while the current is pulling it downstream. When a bass, catfish, sturgeon, pike, or whatever you're trying to catch picks up the bait and moves the line ever so slightly, the line will automatically pop free with a "zing" from where you had wedged it between the toothpick and the rod. This lets the fish run with the bait or swim away somewhere to swallow it.

Most of the time the fish never know that there's a line attached to the bait. This allows the angler plenty of time to set the hook by cranking the bale into gear, which engages the reel's drag system.

Knots

The adage that a chain is as strong as its weakest link holds true for anglers and the knots they tie. If an angler can't tie a good knot, the big one will get away. It won't make a difference if he or she is using the best rod and reel or the heaviest monofilament test line.

Reel and fishing line manufacturers sell their products with instructions on how to attach line to the spool of a reel. Some spools have a knob designed for attaching line using a simple loop knot. Others are made for the line to be threaded around the spool, twisted six or seven times, and threaded back below the junction of the first twist where the line comes around the spool. Like many knots, this one is cinched down so that it's snug to the spool.

Decades ago my father taught me how to snell a hook: a lesson that proved the test of many catfish, bass, and northern pike. We spent many hot afternoons tying knots while we sat in the boat waiting for the coolness of the evening to fall so that we could do some serious fishing. Buck called them ''what-ya-ma-call-it'' knots. We had other names for them like half barrels, blood knots, and catfish loops. We learned it doesn't matter what you call them, as long as you can tie them so that they work. At home, my brother and I would spend 15 minutes before dinner snelling hooks and letting Dad inspect them to see who had the best wraps. Dad just wanted us to learn to tie our own knots so we wouldn't interrupt his fishing.

Clinch Knot

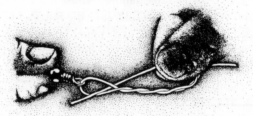

Each knot has a purpose. The clinch knot attaches line from a reel to the ring of a snap swivel or the eyelet of a hook or lure. It won't pull apart when smacked by a pike. If it's tied correctly, it won't snap in the jaws of a flathead catfish. With enough practice, even stone-fingered athletes can snug this knot onto a swivel in two steps, even in the dark. The clinch knot is a prerequisite for plug fishermen and trollers who rely on swivels to keep their line from twisting. It is also used by many fly fishers.

The strength of the clinch knot can be increased by threading the line through the eyelet twice in the initial step. I recommend doing this when going after large fish, such as stripers and muskies, which are capable of popping a normal monofilament knot upon their strike.

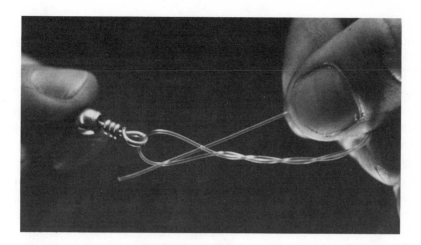

Figure 5.3. To tie a clinch knot, first thread line from a reel or leader through the eyelet of, in this case, a snap-swivel. While holding the loop that you've just formed, wrap the end of the line six or seven times around the portion of the line that is coming from the reel. Then, insert the end of the line back through the hole that was formed between the first wrap and the outer side of the eyelet.   Photo: Michael Macor

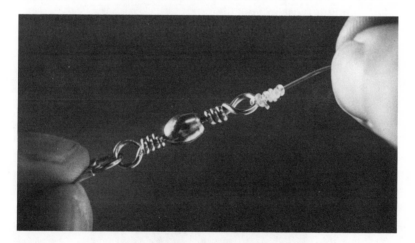

Figure 5.4. Then, moisten with saliva the wrapped portion of the monofilament so that the knot will slide into place easily. The knot is cinched down by holding the end of the line in place so that it doesn't slip out of the hole that you've formed while pulling taut the line from the reel. Be sure to clip off any excess line to about one eighth of an inch from the knot.   Photo: Michael Macor

Loose-Noose Knot

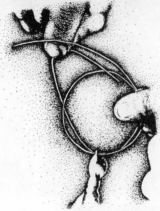

A knot that serves the same purpose of a clinch knot/snap-swivel combination is what I call a loose-noose. I'm sure that it has been called other names as it has been handed down from one professional bass angler to another. It is effective for working jigs, spoons, plastic worms, and even shallow-running plugs because, unlike a metal snap that sometimes kills the action of a lure, it presents the lure in a natural form without putting a twist in your line.

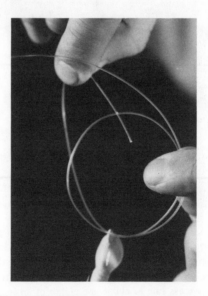

Figure 5.5. To tie a loose-noose knot, first thread the end of the line through the eyelet of a jig or lure. Then, use one hand to form two loops, each the size of a silver dollar, in the portion of the line that comes from the reel, about two or three inches up from where the jig dangles.
Photo: Michael Macor

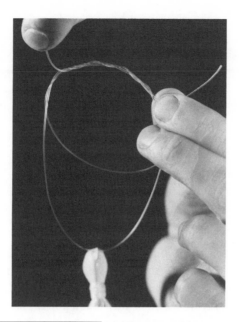

Figure 5.6. Next, while securing the loops with one hand, feed the end of the line first between the loops and then wrap it around both loops four or five times.   Photo: Michael Macor

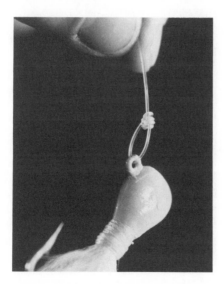

Figure 5.7. With the jig dangling, secure the end line with one hand and the line above the loops with the other. Then, cinch the noose by pulling evenly on the line in both hands in opposite directions. Before tightening the noose, slide it down the line to within one-quarter of an inch from the eyelet.   Photo: Michael Macor

Snelling a Hook

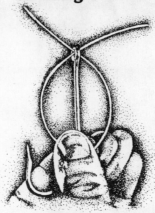

Snelling a hook, as shown in Figures 5.8 through 5.11, requires more coordination of the fingers. An important technique to remember is to hold each wrap in place as it is wound around the shank. Use your ring finger to do this in much the same way that a guitar player holds different chords.

Professionally snelled hooks can be purchased at most bait shops. But ardent bait fishermen snell their own directly to the line to avoid the risk of a salmon or bass damaging a leader or breaking a snap swivel.

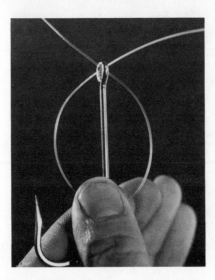

Figure 5.8. Positioning of the hook between the thumb and forefinger is important when snelling a hook. Notice how a loop is formed by the line as it comes through the eyelet in one direction and exits it in the opposite direction.   Photo: Michael Macor

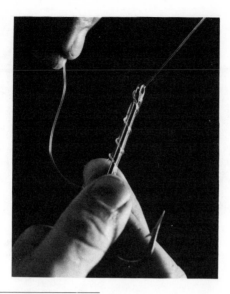

Figure 5.9. While the loop is held in place against the hook's shank, six or seven wraps are made in a clockwise direction. Each wrap is held in place briefly by the middle finger or ring finger of the same hand that is securing the loop against the hook's shank.   Photo: Michael Macor

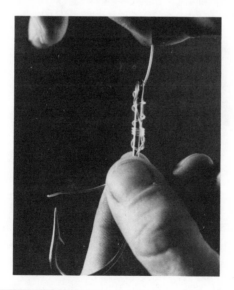

Figure 5.10. After the last wrap has been made, the end of the line is slipped through the loop and held against the shank. Then, while still holding the end of the line against the shank, let the loop free and cinch it up the shank by pulling the line just above where it exits the hook's eyelet. Photo: Michael Macor

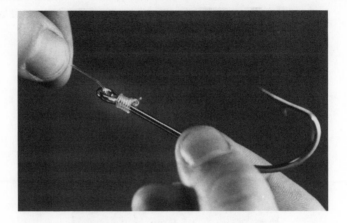

Figure 5.11.   The finished knot has a neat, barrel-like appearance. The
end of the line, which was held against the shank, has been clipped just below the last wrap.   Photo: Michael Macor

Blood Knot

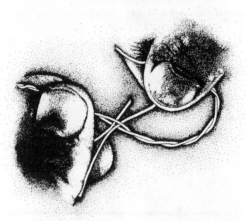

A blood knot is not the only one but perhaps the most common method
of joining two lines that have similar diameters. Either it or the surgeon's
knot is essential to a fly caster who needs to join tippets or attach tapered
leaders.

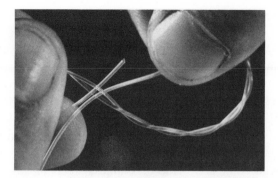

Figure 5.12. To begin a blood knot, take two lines of similar diameter and cross them, holding one line in each hand. Then, take each end and wrap them one at a time, five or six times around the opposite line. Thread the end through the hole where the lines cross.   Photo: Michael Macor

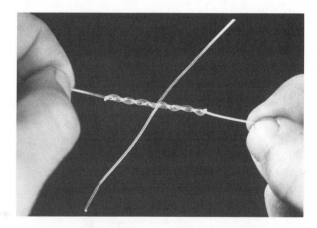

Figure 5.13. Make sure the ends are long enough so that they won't slip back through the hole while each line is pulled taut, evenly, and in opposite directions.   Photo: Michael Macor

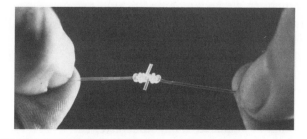

Figure 5.14. The finished blood knot should have the excess ends clipped down and the knot itself should have a neat, barrel-like appearance. Photo: Michael Macor

Hooks

Take a safety pin, snip off the snap part, make a crook-shaped bend near the point, and you'll have a barbless hook without an eyelet.

The advent of wire revolutionized fishing. Wire enabled anglers to fashion hooks with well-honed points. Barbs were added to prevent a hook from slipping. Barbless hooks are used by anglers who plan to release the fish they catch; they prevent serious injury to the fish.

Hooks come in all shapes, sizes, and colors. They can be gold plated or Aberdeen in color and made of stainless steel, nickle, or alloys.

Hooks are evidence that fishing has been around for a while. Some hooks that were fashioned from bones and left by their creators in caves in Norway date back to the Stone Age, more than 5,000 years ago when Vikings navigated the oceans.

Hooks vary according to the shape of the mouth of the fish that they are designed to catch or bait that they are expected to hold. In some instances, shanks are long and crooks are narrow. Small hooks are designed for the mouths of small fish. Hooks with flat or irregular-shaped crooks are made for wide mouths of catfish or the vacuum-like snouts of sturgeon.

Hooks are sized according to numbers. The larger the number, the smaller the hook. A No. 32 hook is a very small hook which is used in fly fishing for trout. A No. 4 hook is a good black bass hook. A No. 1 hook might be used for catfish or large king salmon. Hooks larger than a No. 1 are given an "aught" notation. In this case, the hook size increases with the number. For example, a 6/0 or six-aught hook is bigger than a 5/0. When using staghorn sculpin to catch large striped bass, 7/0 and 8/0 hooks are common. A 14/0 hook is a typical salt water hook made to catch sharks. Most freshwater fish can be caught using hooks smaller than a 1/0.

Double and treble hooks are made for use with plugs and crank baits. Check the points of all hooks before fishing to make sure they are straight, sharp, and have good sticking power. If they're dull, use a file or diamond stone to hone them.

Line

Braided line might be equated to the Studebaker car. There's still some around but few people use it unless they're doing some long-line trolling. The majority of today's anglers relies on monofilament line for fishing needs. Like hooks, line comes in an assortment of colors, thicknesses, and strengths. Some monofilament line appears transparent in water. Other types have high-visibility colors for anglers who depend on watching their line for bites and steering fish on the line away from snags. Use the line best suited to your style of fishing.

Line is rated for its abilities to stretch without breaking and resist abrasion. Limp lines usually have less ability to resist abrasion but stiffer lines, in most instances, are more difficult to cast and have more *memory*. All monofilament lines have some degree of memory, but ones that get crimped or pinched and return to their original form are said to have low memory. Lines with little memory are ideal for rigging fly lines because they remain limp and tangle-free. Stiffer, more rigid lines make for good leader material because they can resist abrasion better than low memory line.

Stiff leaders with test-pound rating comparable to the line are used to sustain the shock of a fish's bite and to prevent frays. Sometimes, when panfishing, anglers will make leaders of lighter test-pound rating than the monofilament to prevent loss of the terminal gear, sinkers, beads, and bobbers, which are positioned above the snap-swivel where the leader is attached. This means that when a crappie takes your bait and wraps your line around a submerged tree or bush, the leader will break first, saving everything above the swivel. Only the hook and leader are lost. What about the fish? Well, you'll just have to rig up again and go after it.

Judging by some world records, fairly large fish can be landed on relatively light test line. Be sure to select the test line that matches the reel specifications and type of fish that you want to catch. If a fish is hooked weighing more than the test-pound rating of your line, rely on your reel's drag system to compensate for the lack of line strength. In other words, loosen the drag.

Fly lines are specially designed to give a fly the proper drift in a lake or stream. They are weighted according to the depth and strength of the current that you want to fish. Some are designed to float on the surface. Others are weighted with different materials shrouded in a slick casing such as Teflon to give the angler a smooth cast. Grease was once commonly used to produce the same effect. Tiny grains of lead are used to weight a super fast sinking line or leadcore line. This type of line is needed to fish extremely fast water or deep holes. Instead of sinking lines, some fly lines are made with a sink tip that keeps the fly under the surface a few feet. Fly lines are tapered to accommodate casting and presentation of the fly.

Shooting lines or "shooting heads" as they are called, are sections of synthetic-coated fly lines about 30 feet long with a loop at the thick end and a stiff, monofilament butt section (about 1-1/2 feet long) attached to the narrowest part of the taper, generally by means of a nail knot that is finally melted to the end of the coated line. A nail knot is a special knot used to join two lines of similar diameter. It is reinforced by several wraps of line that, when tied properly, take on the appearance of line that's been snelled to the shank of a hook. But instead of the line remaining wrapped around the shank or, in this case, a nail, the nail is removed from the knot before it is tightened down. Directions on how to tie nail knots are usually shown on the packages that leaders and fly line come in.

Tapered, monofilament leaders can then be tied to the butt section using a blood knot. Tapered leaders come in different strengths denoted by a number and the letter "X." The bigger the number, the lighter the leader. For example, a 0X leader has a larger diameter than a 1X or 2X. Tapered leaders vary in length from usually 7-1/2 feet (for bass, shad, and not-so-shy fish) to 9-1/2 feet or longer for trout or any fish that you think might be spoofed by having the more visible coated line too close to it. Tapered leaders can also be made using blood knots or surgeon knots to link sections of leader material that decrease in length and test pound rating.

The loop section of a shooting head is there for attaching a running line or "low memory" monofilament line, commonly known as "super shooter" that is carried by the momentum of the heavier, coated section being hauled by the caster. This way, large amounts of "super shooter" can be piled on the water and shot behind the shooting head, resulting in a long-distance cast. The loop allows an angler to change shooting heads quickly to match the conditions of the river.

Sinkers

If the fish you're after is down on the bottom, the best way to present your bait is with an adequate sinker. Sinkers are designed for versatility and efficiency. The best example of this is the split-shot sinker, which can be attached to a line without untying any knots. If more weight is needed to keep your bait in place, just clamp a few more split shots on to give your rig the proper weight.

A barrel-type or egg sinker, shaped like an egg or barrel with a hole in the middle, can be used as a sliding sinker so that the line slides through it. Or it can be used to weight a bobber so that the bobber stands upright in the water.

Another type is the pencil sinker: a long, slender hunk of lead that fits inside a piece of rubber surgical tubing. Pencil sinkers are designed for river fishing so that they'll pull free from the surgical tube if they become snagged.

Bobbers

Some of my first memories of fishing were the hours that I spent watching a bobber. Bobbers are great for beginners who want to learn how to detect the bite of a fish. Different bobbers produce different effects. Some are designed to detect even a minnow getting excited in the presence of a game fish. Others just bob a few times and then go under when a fish strikes. They are usually brightly colored for high visibility on the surface and for night fishing.

Perhaps the most versatile of all bobbers is the long, cigar-shaped slip bobber, also known as the sliding bobber. It has a hole through its center so that the line can slide through it. It is versatile because it can be lobbed long distances like a lure and yet it can be rigged so that the bait will hold at any depth. Because the line can slide through it, slip bobbers allow anglers to reel the fish close to the rod tip for better landing access. This is an advantage over bobbers that must be positioned stationary on the line, thus preventing the fish from being reeled all the way in. A stationary bobber is too big to pass through the rod's cap eyelet.

Slip bobbers require a bead or button and a short piece of rubber band to stop the line that causes the bobber to stand upright. In rigging a slip bobber, first thread a bead or button on the line followed by the bobber, sinker (split-shot or egg-type), snap-swivel, leader, and hook. Tie a rubber band on the line at the depth that you want to fish. If it's 13 feet, then peel out 13 feet of line and snug on a rubber band. Clip off the loose ends of the rubber band so that it looks like a small knot around the line that can pass through the cap eyelet and be reeled onto the spool.

When the bobber and bait rig are tossed, the bobber will remain flat with the water as the bait sinks until the rubber band stops the bead, which in turn stops the bobber and causes it to stand upright. Then, it's a matter of waiting for the bobber to go under or tilt toward the surface, depending on the direction the fish is running with the bait.

Bulb-type or cherry bobbers have some kind of clip mechanism for attaching them to the line. Once attached, the bobber is stationary. This must be taken into consideration when casting the line and landing fish. Cherry bobbers are easy to rig and are ideal for panfish.

When casting bobbers with bait, always try to lob the rig across the water. Lobbing the rig gently creates a smooth impact with the water and avoids yanking apart the tender tissues of a minnow or worm. After all, one function of the bobber is to keep the bait alive and in the vicinity where the fish can find it.

Figure 6.1. (opposite page) With fly rodding, it's the satisfaction that one gets from having presented a fly properly on the stream that makes all the difference.   Photo: Thomas Ovalle

chapter
6

Fishing
techniques

No matter how you slice the bait, it's difficult to become a good angler
without mastering casting skills. Casting is to fishing what pitching is
to baseball. In baseball, if you don't deliver the ball properly, you'll
never strike out a batter. In fishing, if you can't cast with some degree
of accuracy, you'll have a difficult time getting strikes from fish unless, of course, you're lucky. Every aspect of fishing requires some
degree of luck.

Casting

When I think of luck and casting, I think of my friend, Mike Zampa, a curly-haired, former high school football player who is still an avid sports fan. Although an athlete, Mike fell short of his mark when it came to casting. It's not that he was a bad fisherman; nor did he lack desire. In fact, he was fond of fish but admitted one evening while on the way to the lake that his fishing experience was limited to fetching goldfish from his aquarium when it was time to clean the tank.

With his feet planted firmly on a large rock along the shore, Mike attempted a few awkward tosses in the direction of the water. With each cast, he put the plug farther from the shore but never far enough. Seeing a large fish feeding near the surface about 35 yards from where we were standing, I offered to cast his deep-diving plug for him if he would reel it in.

Thanks to luck, the main ingredient in the recipe for angling success, I made one cast with Mike's plug and put it within inches of where we had seen the fish surface last. When I turned the crank handle once to put the reel in gear, that fish, a landlocked striped bass, attacked the plug with such force that I thought it was going to yank the rod from my grip.

Figure 6.2. One way to grip a spinning rod is to straddle the reel stem with the middle fingers. Photo: Thomas Ovalle

"OK," I said to Mike. "You reel it in." Then, I handed him the rod, its tip bobbing with life, and sat down on the rock to watch him battle the only trophy fish of his angling career. What he had wasn't a goldfish from his aquarium but 23 pounds of wild striped bass which ran almost the entire spool of his 12-pound test line to the bottom of a 90-foot hole.

I coached him to keep the rod tip up. Once, I scrambled down the shore to loosen the drag as the bass threatened to snap the line. Mike managed to keep the beast under control until it tired and surfaced on its side within an arm's reach from the edge of the lake. I told Mike to ease it the rest of the way in and then lift it from the water by slipping his forefinger under its gill plate. He accomplished the task while getting only one shoe wet. This amazed me at the time because his knees were still shaking from the battle. He told me later that he realized how valuable casting was to the sport of fishing. "And don't forget luck," I said.

a   b

Figure 6.3 (a and b). A comfortable stance and a slight, forward shift in body weight, as demonstrated from this small boat, make for a smooth delivery in spin casting. When these elements are combined with fluid wrist action and proper timing in the release of line from the index finger, a cast can be placed on line with a target and at the desired distance. It's a matter of body coordination which is learned through practice. Photos: Thomas Ovalle

I learned how to cast in my backyard using a levelwind reel and plugs with no hooks on them which I threw at a hula-hoop lying flat on the lawn. When it was time to break out the hooks and really go after black bass, all that I had to do was envision a hula-hoop surrounding a stump and cast for it. The closer I came to hitting the mark, the better my chances for catching a bass.

Casting with any type of levelwind, spinning, open, or closed-face reel is a matter of matching the weight of the plug with the stiffness of the rod, the friction of the reel, and the size of the line. These factors determine the momentum of your cast. It takes more effort to cast a lightweight lure with a stiff rod and a heavy test line than it does to cast the same lure using a more flexible rod and light test line.

Don't forget that both heavy- and lightweight lures travel farther with the wind at your back than they do by throwing them into or across the wind. Depending on conditions, such as river current and snags, I recommend using 4- to 10-pound test line for most freshwater game fish and 12- to 18-pound test line for most anadromous species, except steelhead for which lighter lines are preferred.

Unlike fly fishing, which depends heavily on movement and positioning of the lower arm, bait casting or spin casting relies more on wrist action. The secret is in the flip of your wrist. A good bait caster can flip a lure from just about any position or style, from overhead casting to sidearm tosses or underhanded flips.

Figure 6.4. When flipping a bait-casting reel, don't forget to thumb the spool to prevent backlashes. Rotating your wrist at the end of your cast, so that the spool's shaft is perpendicular to the ground, allows the spool to turn freely and with consistent speed.   Photo: Thomas Ovalle

Sidearm casts help anglers avoid low-slung branches or trees that hang over a bank. An underhanded flip lets anglers hit a particular spot in a log jam or brushpile without wrapping the line around a branch. Timing is the key to accurate casting. An angler flipping a spinning rod must know the right moment to let the line fly from his or her fingertip. A fly caster must have a knack for timing back casts. Practice in the backyard will improve your casts on the lake.

Sometimes young anglers forget to look behind them when casting because they're so intent on throwing the plug to the other side of the lake. This can result in spilled tackle, tangled lines, and injury to human beings who might have been in the back-cast area. If someone accidentally gets hooked by an errant back cast, immediately administer first aid. Keep a pair of pliers handy. A hook can be removed from an injured person or animal by snipping the shank below the barb and backing the remainder of the hook out the same course that it entered the wound.

Casting is different for lakes and rivers. To cast for fish in a river with stiff currents, anglers should consider the angle that the line will drift after the lure hits the water. If there are snags between you and where you think the fish are, cast downstream so that the drift of your line doesn't get fouled by underwater structures. It's a good idea to wear hip- or chest-waders while stalking streams and rivers. This gives you more accessibility for casting. Fly rodders especially need a larger back-cast area.

Surface plugs of the Hula Popper or Jitterbug varieties that are tossed toward points of land and logs or stumps during early morning and late evening hours can tempt largemouth bass which come to feed in the shallows. When casting these plugs, let them sit for a while before reeling them back in. Give that fish time to locate that "plop" that it just heard. Twitch the popper a bit by waving your rod tip, then work it back on the retrieve.

Be persistent with an area. Let that fish know it's not going to be able to swim in peace until it silences that racket at the surface. Antagonize the fish into biting when casting on the surface.

Fly Rodding

Fly rodding is a game for the stream or lake in which good casts count almost as much as strikes and hook-ups. It's the satisfaction that one

Figure 6.5. Maintain a comfortable grip when using a fly rod. Make sure the reel seat stays flush with the underside of the wrist.   Photo: Thomas Ovalle

gets from having presented a fly properly on the stream that makes all the difference.

A bite or a fish on the line is the reward of all this. Fly fishing demands practice in what's known as roll casting, where the line is plucked from the water by making it roll from the surface with a movement which corresponds to a slight rolling action of the wrist and forearm. The shoulder of the casting arm should remain stationary, allowing the length and limberness of the rod to deliver the cast's momentum.

Think of the rod as an extension of your arm. Unlike spin casting or bait casting, fly casting is a continuous motion in which the rod, not your arms or wrists, delivers the power.

To begin a cast with a fly rod, work out about 20 feet of line from the rod tip, pulling your arm up straight with your elbow tucked into your body. Peel as much out from the reel as you want to cast and let it fall to the side of your casting arm.

In case you've gotten into a bad habit of allowing your elbow to wander away from your torso while you're casting, try it with a dictionary tucked under your armpit. A good fly rodder can make accurate casts without letting the dictionary slip.

Using your body as the center point with your head on an axis in the 12 o'clock position, use your casting arm like the hour hand on a clock to raise the rod back to the 11 o'clock position. Then, drop the rod down to the 2 o'clock position and back again to the 11 o'clock position.

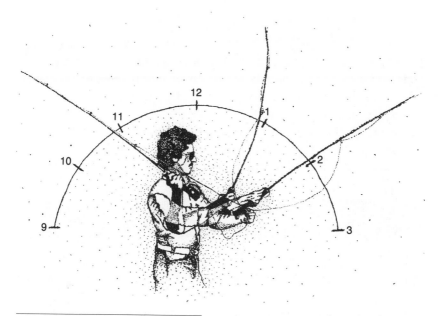

Figure 6.6. Fly casting is a matter of moving the rod in a fluid motion between the 2 o'clock position and the 11 o'clock position on an imaginary clock face in which the angler's head coincides with 12 o'clock.
Illustration: Douglas Klapperich

While standing in a stream, you can work enough line for casting from the rod by stroking the rod tip in the water until the current begins to take it downstream. But when you're standing on dry land, work the line out in little bites, so to speak, by repeating the 11 o'clock to 2 o'clock motion. Be sure to stop the rod at 11 o'clock so that after the line goes back in a loop, it straightens out without sagging or falling. Then, when the line is finally straight behind you, bring the rod smoothly forward to the 2 o'clock position. As the line begins to lie down on the water, follow through with your rod tip so that the fly lands on the surface. Then raise the rod tip a bit so that the fly has a drag-free drift. Don't steer the fly with the rod. Rather, present it to the fish naturally as if there weren't a string attached to it.

Again, as in other types of casting, timing is essential. In fly rodding a rule of thumb on the back cast is to hesitate for a count of "one-one thousand" before the line is shot forward and released from the grip of your thumb and index finger.

Long casts are made by a technique called *double hauling* in which more line is worked out during repeated hauls of the line before it is released. Some anglers keep neat loops of fly line secured by their teeth so that when momentum builds up in the cast, the angler can open his mouth to release the extra line so that it shoots free untangled. To paraphrase one old saying, don't bite off more than you can cast. As your ability increases, you'll be able to clutch more excess line between your teeth. Remember, the weight of the fly line must correspond to the length and flexibility of the rod.

It is equally important to consider the conditions under which you're casting. When casting into the wind, you'll have to bring the rod farther down than the 2 o'clock position in order to get the line to lie down.

Figure 6.7 (a-d). To cast with a fly rod, think of the rod as an extension of your arm. Pluck the line from the water by raising the rod to the 11 o'clock position; then stop it and let the line straighten behind you before lowering the rod back to the 2 o'clock position. Time the release of the line between the two positions so that it will carry through with the rod's forward momentum. Photos: Thomas Ovalle

Conversely, with the wind blowing against your back, you'll want to shorten the back cast, say to 12 o'clock. In addition you'll want to apply more power to the back cast and less power to the forward cast. Be sure to duck if a gust comes up and drives the fly toward the back of your head and ears. Always make sure that no one is standing behind you and that there's ample room for a smooth back cast.

Drift Fishing

Many anglers catch fish by casting from a boat that is drifting with the current or the wind. An electric trolling motor, especially one clamped to the front of a bass boat and equipped with a foot pedal for directional operation, is very useful for holding a steady drift in a reservoir. A pair of oars will accomplish the same task but with a lot more effort and noise. Paddling a canoe might be more quiet.

The object in casting while adrift is to work a large stretch of shoreline as the boat moves slowly. In states where fishing with two rods is allowed, drift fishing is an excellent way to put a bobber out the back with a minnow about six or seven feet under it or even shallower. A second rod is used to cast with the drift. Sometimes a fish will follow a lure toward the boat then spot the injured minnow and go for it. This works well on bass, walleye, pike, and large crappie. Sometimes a catfish will smack a bait that's drifted in this manner.

The technique of back oaring is a standard method for taking steelhead, silver, and king salmon from rivers in the Pacific Northwest and Great Lakes regions. It involves one or two anglers positioned in the front or bow of a boat with their lines in the water, carried downstream by the river's current. The oarsman is seated near the middle or sometimes in the bank (or stern) of the boat. By rowing backwards, the oarsman can hold the boat's position in the river, while at the same time controlling the position of the lines by maneuvering the boat from one side of the river to the other, gradually working each hole as the current carries the boat downstream. The object is to run Hot Shots and Flatfish-like lures about 35 yards downriver of a drift boat: a flat-bottomed, high-gunneled vessel that's designed for three people. Two are positioned on each side of the bow seat with an oarsman at the stern who keeps the boat in line with the current and always pointing downstream. The anglers simply let the current take their lures ahead of the boat about 40 or 50 feet downriver where they remain while the oarsman traverses the river from side to side. The lures, which dig into the current, produce action from the flow of water rushing by them.

Trolling

Trolling a river or reservoir in a boat powered by either an electric motor or small outboard motor is a popular method for catching trout in large, high mountain lakes. It is also a common method for canvassing unfamiliar northern lakes or Midwest reservoirs for bass, walleye, pike, landlocked striped bass, and Great Lakes salmon. Trolling is commonly used to rouse lazy lunkers from deep holes and weed beds in spring-fed lakes during the peak of summer.

Depending on the species and the water temperature (remember that when it's colder fish are less active), a rule of thumb for trolling speeds is to troll only fast enough to give the lure a natural swimming action. Spinners should be trolled very slowly, preferably attached to a snap-swivel to avoid twisting the line. Jigs, plugs, and spoons can be worked so fast that the rod tip rhythmically bounces as the line drags through the water. Once a speed is found that produces a strike from a fish, mark that speed by putting a pencil mark on the motor's throttle if it's a till-steer type so that speed can be found again when trolling resumes. With enough experience, you'll be able to set the speed just by listening to the motor's pitch. For inboard-outboard engines, a standard trolling speed is about 900 revolutions per minute, which can be easily set using a tachometer.

Following a zigzag course while trolling changes the speed of a lure as it swings through the curves. This causes a more varied action from the lure and allows it to cover a cross-section of the lake or river. Zigzagging a boat on the troll is particularly effective while using a lead-headed jig in combination with an action lure, such as a broken-back, deep-diving minnow imitation. Trolling combination lures requires a spreader rig: a wire, clothes hanger-type device that keeps two lures, a jig and a plug, apart from each other as they are pulled through the water in tandem. The game fish sees the plug chasing the jig, thinks it's a free meal, and tries to snatch it away from the plug. Sometimes the fish will try to take advantage of the plug. Either way, you can catch a fish.

In areas where fish are known to hold in schools, either suspended in open water or holding near underwater structures, lures should be trolled in a figure eight pattern. By a figure eight pattern, envision the trolling area as a big race track. Instead of driving your boat in ovals around this track, follow a figure eight course in which the "X" portion of the "8" is where you've either caught a fish or had a strike. The figure eight trolling method will take your boat in two different directions each time a lap is completed. Sometimes it's the direction in which a lure is presented over an underwater structure that makes the fish strike.

When trolling shallow water, let out about 60 to 80 yards of line attached to a subsurface lure. This allows time for fish to regroup after the boat trolls over them or the line is dragged through them. After a school of fish separates, you want to have the lure waiting in front of them when they regroup. The more line that's out, the more time it gives the fish to regroup.

Still Fishing

Still fishing refers to the angler who has located fish time after time at a certain spot and anchors there to fish with an appropriate bait. The object is to wait for the fish to come by.

Recalling a previously mentioned technique, the toothpick trick, the object is to get the fish to run with the bait until it's had a chance to swallow it. In some angling circles, this is what still fishing is all about. A conventional bait casting reel set on free spool accomplishes the same objective, but you might have to adjust the spool tension by tightening the knob located on the side of the reel so that tides or river currents don't drag the line downstream. Be sure to leave it loose enough, however, so that a fish can't detect tension on the line when it finds the bait.

Sometimes a fish will pick up a bait and swim toward the boat or maybe swim at an angle from the boat. It might even swim 10 yards and stop, then take off again after it has positioned the bait fish headfirst in its mouth. Whatever the case, it's important to pay attention to the direction in which the fish is swimming. Then, when it's time to set the hook, you can point the rod in that direction and gradually reel up until the line tightens. Immediately come back hard, keeping the rod tip high while driving that hook into the fish's throat or lips.

It's fun to catch fish this way but it's also a waiting game. When you see that line peeling off for the first time and you turn the crank handle, setting the drag in gear, and your rod tip bounces with life, you'll know that patience pays off and the toothpick trick or some variation of it is the slickest way to catch a bass or catfish since man invented the hook.

There are other methods of still fishing. Many times anglers invent their own methods to match the habits of a particular species or to adjust to a particular condition. Half of the sport of fishing is using your own ingenuity to outsmart fish. An angler must be a creative person who is willing to experiment with different methods.

A common tactic in still fishing is to use a *tight line*. In this method, a weight is placed about 12 inches or more from the hook so that it sits right on the bottom or just above it. All slack is reeled up after the cast to keep the line tight. This way, even the slightest nibble will bounce the rod tip. The angler sets the hook at the first opportunity after the bite is detected.

If you're having trouble detecting bites while still fishing, use some type of bobber setup. A slip bobber allows a bait to be positioned at any depth with no difficulty casting it or reeling in a fish. Fixed bobbers such as a cherry bobber or stick bobber limit how much line can dangle and still be properly tossed. In the case of fish such as pike, which need time to scale their prey before swallowing it, let the bobber go under twice. The first time, it stays down for a long time while the pike is scaling the bait. The next time the bobber comes up the pike will be trying to swim away with its prize. That's the time to set the hook.

Open water fish will locate bait anywhere from a few inches to several feet below a bobber, depending on the depth at which they're swimming and the water temperature. If, for example, it was discovered that largemouth bass are suspended in water that's 58 °F, then it's a good idea to sink a thermometer to various depths until 58° is located. Set your bobber to fish that depth.

Bottom feeders such as catfish should be fished with a bobber rig that holds bait right off of the bottom. If a submerged bush tops out at 6 feet below the surface, set your bobber at 5-1/2 feet; that's where crappie and panfish will be more apt to locate your bait as it is just above the bush.

Be flexible with your methods of taking fish. Experiment with casting and variations of bait fishing. Learn how to cast a fly rod and flip a levelwind reel. As in any other sport, practice makes perfect.

Figure 7.1. (opposite page) Early morning light silhouettes a lunker bass that was caught when it moved into the shallows to feed. Photo: Michael Macor

chapter
7

Fishing conditions

Bass can make you humble. So can wind and big waves.

"You had no business being there under conditions like that," scorned Jack Berman, a veteran sailor of roily waters. More than once in the 25 years that he fished every Monday, Wednesday, and Friday morning on Suisun Bay did he run across foul weather. He's seen the rollers swell over the gunnels and he's high-tailed it back to the docks when the flag was blowing straight out.

Once, a cabin cruiser chomped his 12-foot aluminum boat in half while going full blast back to Pierce Harbor. Jack ended up losing his rods and reels and even his fish, but he lived to tell about it.

111

Jack understood what we had experienced when he heard about Terry Robin and me. There was nothing unusual about that Tuesday morning when we hitched up the 12-1/2-foot aluminum Bass-O-Matic to the back of the pickup and headed for the river to a place where it widened out before dumping into Honker Bay. I had taken the normal precautions: I checked with the National Weather Service for the forecast, which called for winds from the southwest increasing in the afternoon. It didn't sound different from the previous Sunday morning when we anchored the Bass-O-Matic in the same hole and practically knocked the stripes off the linesided bass, landing three in the first hour of fishing—two at 20 pounds and one at 28 pounds.

It must have been that temptation, that desire to catch more bass that sent me sailing back to the hole with Terry on Tuesday.

When we reached the Bait Shop at McAvoy Harbor, the "bait lady," Beverly Laine, let me look through a pair of binoculars to see the 4-foot tide smoothing along the entrance to the harbor.

The weather seemed all right then, with the winds coming from the southwest. Ron Sittinger, a knowledgeable skipper in that part of the delta, had taught me a few things about the wind and the waters there.

"Whenever it comes up from the north or northwest," he said, "get off the pond."

Terry and I fished about three hours in the Honker Bay hole, a place we secretly called "China Cove." We anchored in seven feet of water. It was choppy, but not unlike the previous Sunday morning. I even told Terry that I thought the wind was good for fishing because it whipped the water full of more oxygen which stimulated the bass.

In the first hour of fishing, we caught one 8-pound striper, a small one by standards in that part of the country. Two other times we had fish on. One, which we thought was a sturgeon, snapped Terry's line.

Though it was sunny and breezy, Terry jokingly mentioned while netting the fish that the water felt warm. "Hey, we ought to go swimming," he laughed.

An hour went by and it was noon, the time I said the big ones would come by, judging by the tide. Terry dozed off in the middle seat where we both had sat during the morning tide. Anchored the way it was, the boat made less noise as its bow rode over the crest of the waves while the stern whipped behind in the troughs.

Once in a while, an outgoing roller would lift the back end a foot or so but the Bass-O-Matic always rode, taking in an occasional splash which we'd bail every half hour.

It was about 12:30 when I looked over my left shoulder and saw that the wind had shifted to the northwest. Recalling what Sittinger had said, I immediately picked up my rod and began reeling in. Before I got the bait in, a 5-foot-tall wall of water swelled around that little boat and tossed it about like a toothpick caught in an ocean wave. Immediately it knocked me back toward the outboard motor where I landed with one arm over the side.

The next wave slammed over the stern and swamped the Bass-O-Matic in a fraction of a second. Water from the crest crashed over the gunnels like a truck dumping tons of sand into a little sandbox.

It took just seconds for the boat to fill up with water causing it to list to one side with its bow still up. Dazed and clinging to the bow, Terry and I immediately began treading water. We watched as one flotation cushion drifted by, keeping pace with the wind. It headed for the shoreline about a mile away. I grabbed the other one and asked Terry if he was all right. He nodded, "yes," but I could tell that he was having trouble making it to the point of the overturned bow, the only part of the boat that remained above water thanks to a pocket of air. I offered an outstretched arm, which he promptly accepted, then with my other hand I paddled the two of us to a safer part of the capsized hull.

"Stay with the boat," I told him, as we watched the last seat cushion float farther away. I decided to swim the 75 yards or so to retrieve it, a task I accomplished with my tennis shoes on. But when I reached the cushion, I kicked off the sneakers and swam back to Terry who was groping for air. I slid the cushion under his chest and told him to relax.

Why was this 20-year-old athlete—a guy who runs five miles a day and knows how to swim—having so much trouble treading water?

Then it struck me. "Have you still got your shoes on?" I asked. Not only did he have his shoes on but they were thick-soled logging boots. It was as if he had shackles on his ankles.

Bobbing up and down while trying to brace himself on the overturned bow, Terry managed to get his boots off. He handed them to me, one at a time. I used the laces to lash them to the D-ring on the bow. As we jostled with the submerged boat, trying to right it, my fly rod bolted loose from underneath. Grabbing the rod, I snipped the line and slid it tip first through the bootstraps on Terry's boots, dangling from the bow.

Recuperating a bit, we shed some of our heavy clothes and water-logged jackets and proceeded to survey the damage around the perimeter of the boat. We tried with no success to right it, only shaking loose the floor boards and the gasoline tank, all of which shot to the surface. We decided to unsnap the anchor and drift with the boat, hoping the strong wind and five feet of incoming tide would beach us or at least put us in shallow water.

The plan worked for about 200 feet but the weight of the 18-horse-power outboard motor, a 12-volt battery, and assorted fishing gear lugged us down. We both felt cramps coming on.

It was pointless to try to salvage the boat. So, using the cushions to support us, we swam side-by-side two feet apart, stroking and back kicking for the tule-flocked shoreline. We stopped twice along the way to relax our legs and prevent cramps in the cold water. Only after we rested did we head in again. We didn't panic but kept telling each other how nice it would be to sit down on dry land with warm clothes and eat a charbroiled steak dinner.

Terry's watch indicated that we had been swimming, wrestling with the boat, and treading water for nearly two hours. We finally reached the shoreline after wading for about 100 yards through the shallows. We had smiles on our faces. We slapped our hands and rejoiced that we had survived the ordeal.

We took an inventory at a makeshift hut which we had constructed out of driftwood and a slab of plywood. We had one soggy, tide book, a Bic lighter, a waterproof wristwatch, and a pair of fingernail clippers. It took about five minutes for the lighter to dry out in the wind before we could build a fire. The fire served two purposes: To dry out our clothes and to attract any helicopters, planes, or boats in the area.

There were no boats in sight; the bay at that point had become un-navigable. While Terry kept the fire going, I headed for a point of land on the channel about a mile away. My intention was to flag down a boat that might be trying to make it back to the harbor. We were too far back in the tules to be spotted from a distance.

The hike to the point was no stroll along a beach. I marched through knee-deep water and a dense growth of cattails. The tide was coming in fast. Fortunately, one of my gray sneakers washed up in my path; I found the other one a few hundred feet away. Though soggy, the shoes aided my trek by keeping the sharp, bamboo-like shoots from piercing my tender feet.

I headed for a set of wooden pilings strung together by cables to prevent boats from mistakenly entering a hidden slough. The tide was nearly in and it was too deep to walk the shore. I started to swim again, occasionally grasping the cables to pull me from piling to piling. I hauled a bright yellow rainsuit that had washed up with my shoes. When I reached the last piling, I climbed on top and saw that it would be impossible to go any farther because of the tide and the wind.

I stood like a big seagull, perched atop the piling when I heard the whine of an outboard motor. It was Gizzy Gallie in his 16-foot camouflaged duck boat trying to reach the club house on the opposite shore. It was so rough on the bay that he had ducked around the corner to find a route less plagued by the wind.

Giz saw me waving that yellow rain suit and idled his way to my location. I hopped aboard, we made two swipes at locating the Bass-O-Matic and then worked our way toward Terry's makeshift hut. Terry waded to the boat; Giz worried that a wave would swamp us if we took the craft all the way in.

After a blockbuster ride back to the bait shop, Tom Laine loaned us some dry clothes, and his wife, Bev, fetched some hot grub. The next morning one of the veteran Honker Bay anglers, Fred Brown, saw my fly rod bobbing from the bow of the Bass-O-Matic while he was fishing the flats. A few buddies with bigger boats took me back to the spot and we winched the sunken craft out, sacrificing the motor and most of the gear to the deep mud.

Yep. Bass and big waves can make a fellow humble. There is some risk involved in all sports. Only those who don't panic live to tell of the lessons learned.

Wind

Wind can turn an angler's dream into a nightmare, oftentimes in an instant. To some degree wind can be beneficial to those who respect it and know how to use it to their advantage. Whether it be Honker Bay, California, or Leech Lake, Minnesota, wind always makes for bigger whitecaps over large or shallow bodies of water. Currents compound the effect.

A gentle breeze parallel to the shore is an ideal condition for a pair of anglers in an aluminum boat to cast for largemouth bass. An oar or paddle is all that's needed to keep a canoe aligned with the bank.

Drift casting with a breeze is one of the most quiet and effective methods for sneaking up on fish. With no noise from a gasoline engine, drift fishing with oars has proven to be a natural method of catching fish.

Ice Fishing

For decades, anglers in the northern Great Lakes areas of the United States have relied on spearing fish for both survival and sporting purposes. They would fashion a minnow from a buoyant stick the size of a broom handle and paint it in patterns of a sucker or young perch. They'd hollow out the underside of this dummy minnow and fill the resulting cavity with lead or a heavy metal. Then they'd tie a string on the top center of this homemade plug and lower it through a hole in the ice until it sat suspended off the bottom. No hooks were attached to the plug.

The idea was to jiggle this brightly-colored plug in the underwater spotlight caused by the winter sun piercing the hole, one that was drilled with a spiral-shaped auger. The anglers worked the plug like a puppet on a string. The lead weight made it sit upright yet the wood was buoyant enough to give it a lifelike bounce. Out of curiosity, big northern pike will slowly investigate the activity by swimming right up to it and staring at it with their elongated snouts.

To detect this activity in shallow water (10 to 12 feet), anglers enhanced their viewing abilities through the ice hole by cracking egg shells and dropping the white pieces through the hole where they formed a plain, mosaic background on the floor of the lake. When a pike came in a clear line of fire with its body in contrast to the white surface below, the angler would chuck a spear hoping to stick it long enough to pull the fish in hand over fist by a cord attached to the spear's tail.

This may sound like a primitive method of catching fish but it is a perfect example of an angler who catches fish by adjusting his methods to the conditions. Again, the key is to think like fish so that you can create a condition that will attract them to a place where you're waiting for them to come by.

The first thing every ice fisherman should do is check the thickness of the ice where he or she plans to fish. No one wants to get caught on thin ice in the middle of Minnesota in January. It makes a difference whether you're fishing a pond or a lake, or especially a river or stream. Running water means thin ice at lower than normal temperatures.

One essential tool for every ice angler is a spud, ice chisel, or auger. Since casting is not an essential skill in ice fishing, a short rod called a *tip-up* is all that's needed to lower line through a hole. The length of the rod is kept short enough to allow the angler to monitor tip action at the ice hole. Ice fishing rods are balanced like a teeter-totter; when a fish strikes, the rod tip swings down, allowing the angler time to pick up the rod in a gloved hand and set the hook. Oftentimes, fish are landed from deep holes by pulling the line in hand-over-fist following a strike.

Night Fishing

Night fishing at Occoquan Reservoir in northern Virginia is an orchestra of crickets and whippoorwills, with an occasional frog chiming in. All of these sounds are evidence of the life that abounds in a lake nestled in a hardwood forest. The fish are on the prowl as well.

A frog jumping from a rock, causing a ruckus at the surface, is enough to entice any largemouth or smallmouth bass into biting. Surface plugs such as Hula Poppers or small fly poppers can simulate the action of a frog plodding through the water. A popper is allowed to sit on the water momentarily after it's been cast. The tentacles on its rubber skirt dangle while the plug sits motionless. A bass lurking below sees this and often strikes before the angler actually begins to work the plug. After it's allowed to sit for a few seconds, pop the plug by twitching the rod tip. Wind up slack as the plug swims toward you, twitching it sporadically during the retrieve.

There are some important things to consider before taking on the wilderness at night. I usually carry a flashlight but seldom use it except when light is needed to thread a line through an eyelet of a hook or a lure. Flashlights have a tendency to ruin night vision which is vital to anyone who must concentrate on a rod tip or navigate the surroundings. An angler can see best at night by constantly rolling his eyes back and forth, allowing the pupils to detect different shades in the darkness. The darker areas become hard silhouettes and are essential for determining depth perception. You need depth perception in order to cast a fly or lob a bait. You especially need it to find your way to the fishing hole, whether it be over land or on the water.

Catfishing at night is a popular sport in the lower lakes of the Blue Ridge Mountains. Its popularity extends to the mountain areas of Kentucky, Tennessee, and West Virginia. Big channel cat and flathead catfish become very active as the sun sets, often feeding through the night while moving into the shallows from the deep holes where they hide during broad daylight. These adult catfish, weighing 5 to 10 pounds and not uncommonly over 30 pounds, fall prey to the bait angler who uses the right bait and the right technique at the right hour of the day. Moonlit nights (particularly a full moon according to my records) seem to be the best time to use big shiny minnows in a lake or river where channel catfish feed naturally on the same type of baitfish. Sucker minnows fished below a slip bobber at the edge of a pool in a meandering river have produced some outstanding channel cats. The same method works well in a lake while fishing from a boat anchored at the edge of a deep hole caused by a point of land. The advantage of using the slip bobber setup is that you can lob large minnows with a medium action rod and you can fish that minnow at exactly the depth where the fish are, regardless of whether it is 6 inches or 16 feet. A slip bobber fished at night also allows you to drift bait in an area. When live minnows are used at night, oftentimes they'll find the fish for you as they swim aimlessly around searching for a log or branch under which to hide. They also have a tendency to seek shallow water.

In some states, it's legal to use a trot line or jug line to catch catfish at night. There are rules for setting them and monitoring them. These methods are essentially a way to harvest catfish from mountain lakes and reservoirs. Trot lining or jug fishing is, however, a way of locating fish and figuring out where they go at night. There are two types of trot lines. A set line is set from a fixed point on the bank to a weight or float anchored in the lake. The true trot line, however, is often strung between two points across a cove and is run or trotted by the fisherman. Jug lines consist of plastic jugs, 10-foot leader, hook, and minnow. Fish attack the minnow and get tired out trying to pull the jug under. Jug lines are retrieved at dawn by two anglers in a canoe or small boat.

Figure 8.1. (opposite page) Jim Wright of Canada demonstrates the art of playing a salmon in an Alaskan stream.   Photo: Keith Rogers

chapter 8

Playing the big one

It was twilight on the reservoir when I saw the water swell about 15 yards from where I had just pitched a minnow-imitation plug, painted blue on top and silver underneath, and patterned after a fingerling rainbow trout.

When I heard the splash, my heart jumped with a sudden surge of adrenaline which throbbed through my body and made it difficult to maintain a rhythm during the retrieve.

It was obvious that a big fish was feeding. A six-inch trout blipped from the water and skittered across the surface, as if it were trying to grow wings and fly away from the mammoth she-fish. Suddenly, the striped bass that had been tailing it broke the surface and thrashed about wildly, trying to corral the little trout and devour it in one cannibalistic swirl.

As I reeled the hefty plug to the tip of my fiberglass rod, things became still. I flipped the bale and fired another cast about nine yards beyond the spot where a ring of hula-hoop-size ripples reverberated from the bass's downward journey.

"Kerrsplash!" Another striper surfaced in the distance near the base of a rocky point. Obviously, a school of big fish had moved into the shallows to feed.

I continued to crank the lure at a quick, erratic pace. I must have tossed it eight or nine times, canvasing a pie-shaped section of the lake in front of me. Each time the line would peel from the spool and settle on the water 35 or 40 yards away.

On one toss to about the 11 o'clock position, the line became stiff. Its slack, curved appearance began to straighten as if it were attached to a lead weight descending to the bottom. Instantly the drag system on my reel began to ring out a ratchety song into the stillness of the evening. In a split second, I released the crank handle and flipped the lever that locked the drag in place. It continued to make a grinding sound as my 7-1/2-foot rod bowed with each lunge the fish made. The fish fought furiously for its life.

Fumbling for the knob that loosened the drag, I managed to find it and spin it a couple of quarter-turns counterclockwise. The fish shot upward and wallowed on the surface before it made what seemed like a never-ending dive to the bottom.

It was like trying to control a mad dog on a long leash. I tried to horse the fish away from sharp rocks but my 15-pound test line twanged with tension. I decided to let the bass run where it wanted.

With the line piercing the water at a 45-degree angle, the bass made a southward turn toward a cove lined with brush and steep banks. Halfway there, it surfaced again, shooting from below like a missile launched from a submarine. Time seemed to stop when it tail-walked across the water and shook its head violently, trying to rid the plug that dangled from the corner of its mouth. It dived again and ripped out another 30 yards. Then the line went limp.

I cranked up the slack rapidly, hoping with each turn that I'd feel its massive body tugging away. With about 50 feet to go, I detected a bobbing sensation below. The bass was still on the line and swimming toward me faster than I could reel. When it neared the place where

I was standing, my silhouette must have spoofed it back to the deep. It seemed like hours had passed as I watched line peel from the reel. In reality, I jostled with the bass for 10 to 15 minutes from one side of the cove to the other.

After it spent a few more minutes seesawing back and forth in the deep hole, the bass set my drag with a powerful lunge; then it slowly began to tire. I worked it closer to where I planned to land it, from a perch on a large, flat rock. The bass wagged along one side of the bank and sauntered back again. I winched it closer, foot-by-foot, until the silver side of its 40-inch body flashed in front of me. Two feet from the bank, the striper leaned on its side, permitting me to ease it the rest of the way to within an arm's reach.

I raised my rod tip high with one hand, and with the other thrust two fingers under its gill plate and plucked it from the water. Being careful not to wipe the slime from its body, I laid the fish flat across three moss-covered boulders. The best I could tell, the bass was in fact a female, her belly plump with eggs. She remained still while I slackened the line and spent a few seconds trying to dislodge the hooks from her cigar-size lip. One was embedded so deep that I took out my pocket knife and quickly cut back the tissue a bit so the hook's barb could slide out.

The bass twitched when it felt free of the lure. Its dorsal fin fanned out and threatened to pierce my leg with its sharp points. She was too tired and too fat to flap wildly on the bank. I set my rod down and used two hands to gently lift its hulking body from the mossy cushion of the rocks. I kneeled to the water's edge and pointed her head toward the lake. Her gold eyes blinked. The chance to escape revived her. I held her at the meaty part of her tail and submerged her in the lake.

Figure 8.2. To release a fish, work it back and forth in the water by its tail until it regains enough strength to break free from your grip.
Photo: Marian Green

Then I wagged her body back and forth, trying to work the tension out of her muscles. Water rushed through her gills as I pushed her out and pulled her back. After a few seconds, her gills expanded and contracted in rhythm. She held her natural upright position without listing to one side. She began to get some of her old spunk back and struggled to free her tail from my grasp, but I held tight. When she revived to the point where I could hardly keep her from swimming away, I released her; she shot back to the deep from where she had come.

I propped one foot on a nearby boulder and thought about how much fun it had been playing that monster from the lake. The sight of her suspended in the air, balanced on her tail with water spraying all around was something I'd never forget. I picked up my rod, untwisted the line, and began casting again for another striped bass. At least I knew there was one big one left. And maybe, if the water got high enough in the creek, she'd find her way to a fast current and drop her eggs. Then, with any luck, there would be a few more bass to battle.

Pointers on Landing a Fish

Playing a lunker fish until it can be landed and released unharmed should be the ultimate goal of every sport fisherman. There are a few fundamentals to remember during the excitement of a fight. Always keep your rod tip high. Never point it in a direction that will give a fish enough slack to shake a hook loose. Be prepared to reel rapidly as a fish swims toward you. Again, keep that rod tip up.

The technique in tiring out large fish is to reel down and pull back. By pulling back, you gain ground on the fish, but it is important to reel down immediately to avoid putting slack in the line. Don't horse a fish by pumping the rod or shaking it. Let the line capacity of your reel work for you as you gradually get an idea of how big the beast is compared to your line's test rating. Make sure that all your hand and arm movements are fluid and smooth in order to keep constant pressure on the hook's point.

Let the reel's drag system tire a fish out. In the case of a fly rod, let the rod's action assume the brunt of the battle. Use the flex of the rod and whatever braking action is available from the reel and your grip on the line. Try to make the river work for you instead of for the fish.

Whether you're playing a mighty muskie or a pan-sized bluegill, all hooked fish are wild animals fighting for their lives. They'll try anything to get free. Once landed, they'll attempt to ward you off with their horns or spines. Some species get so slimy, they're almost impossible to handle. Large sturgeon have been known to literally tear up boats as they thrash about uncontrolled on the deck.

All fish have some built in mechanism that allows the angler some degree of control over it. You subdue a black bass by inserting your thumb into its mouth and depressing its tongue. This paralyzes the fish briefly so that hooks can be removed and the fish can either be released or put into a live box. Fish such as pike and muskie have rows of needle sharp teeth which prevent anglers from paralyzing them by depressing their tongues. The proper way to subdue a pike or any fish with this type of teeth is to pinch the base of its eye sockets with a firm grip by a thumb and forefinger.

Once tired, large striped bass can be plucked from the water by lifting them at the intersection of the gill plates on the underside of their bodies.

When a net is used, always lead a fish into it head first. Never show the fish the net until you are ready to bring it in and it's tired out enough to come in without causing too much racket. Fish become fairly excited at the sight of a net.

If a net is not available and you are fighting a large fish from a boat, don't panic. Pull in the anchor, or better yet, tie it off with a float and let the fish pull the boat. This tires a fish fairly well and lets you work them toward the shore, enabling you to get out of the boat and land the fish by beaching it.

Once, while fishing from shore, I had a striped bass run almost all the line off my spool. Seeing there were only a few feet left, I held the rod above my head keeping one hand on the crank handle as I walked along the bank in the direction the fish wanted to go. After seesawing up and down the shore for about 300 yards, the bass came under control where I could beach it on a sand bar.

Check to make sure the reel's drag is set according to the test line. For spinning reels it should be set for 40% of the tensile strength of the line. Be ready to adjust it quickly if the fish appears to outweigh the line's test pound rating. Never tighten a drag beyond the breaking point of the line, but don't have it so loose that you can't set a hook.

Using 10-pound monofilament line, I once successfully battled a 43-pound striped bass. The fight lasted 40 minutes even with the fish pulling a 16-foot boat across the current. It took Joey Pallotta five hours to battle his world record 468-pound sturgeon. Don't be in too big of a hurry to land too big of a fish.

A key element in landing any fish is setting the hook properly. To set a hook doesn't necessarily mean that you have to rear back and yank the fish's lips off. Sometimes this is the case with large fish that have tough jaws and throats; more often than not, setting the hook means sticking the point in the fish with short but powerful jabs, making sure that the rod tip is kept high. This way, the hook has a better chance at sticking even if the fish makes a sudden run back toward you or decides to shoot to the surface.

Most members of the trout family have relatively soft mouths. Anglers battling brook trout in New England or West Coast fishermen fighting chinook on their way upriver to spawn should never forget that hooks will pull free from the soft mouths of these bionic trout, especially if the hooks are yanked.

Figure 8.3. Marian Green of Livermore, California, caught this 25-pound landlocked striped bass from Lake Del Valle while trolling a deep-diving plug that resembled a rainbow trout. Photo: Keith Rogers

A striped bass should run with a live bullhead or mudsucker until the hook can be set with enough force to embed it in its throat or lips. Again, keep the rod tip high to make the hooks stick.

Many times pike, walleye, and bass will set the hook by themselves just from the force of their strike. Don't rip the plug or spinner away from a striking fish with such force that it sprays water into the air. Be certain to keep tension on the line. This makes it more difficult for a fish to shake free from a hook.

Above all, keep the rod tip up and remember to be patient.

Glossary

Angler: One who uses hook and line to catch fish.

Backlash: A tangled mess of line around a fishing reel's spool, which occurs when a caster forgets to thumb the spool and it rotates out of control.

Back-oaring: The act of rowing a boat so that it holds its place in a river's current to allow anglers to work the river's holes and structures.

Barb: A sharp protrusion beneath the point of a hook that keeps the hook from slipping through a fish's lip or throat after the point becomes embedded during a hook-up.

Bobber: A flotation device that is attached to a fishing line to suspend bait at a desired depth and is usually made of wood, cork, foam, or plastic; vibrations of the bobber indicate when a fish is biting.

Conventional reel: An open-face fishing reel that retrieves line on a relatively long spool, usually equipped with a star-type drag system; when a conventional reel is disengaged, the line must be thumbed to prevent backlash.

Drag: This mechanism of a fishing reel is used to tire a fish. The drag on bait-casting reels can be tightened by rotating (clockwise) the star-shaped wheel on the side of the reel. Tightening the drag too much can break a line during hook-ups with large fish. Spinning reels usually have a knob-type drag adjustment.

Fly: An artificial bug tied around a hook to represent some stage of development of an insect or a young hatch of bait fish.

Graph: A sonar, electronic fish locator that plots individual fish and groups of bait fish on a rotating, paper chart; the word is short for "graphic recorder."

Guides: Stationary eyelets of descending diameters, which are wrapped to the rod in a tunnel-like arrangement and used to guide the line from the reel to the cap eyelet positioned at the rod's tip.

Hook: A curved metal pin with a point and an eyelet to which a line or leader can be attached.

Jig: A lead-headed lure, usually with a stiff skirt for vertical jigging.

Knot: Standard method for attaching fishing line to hooks, lures, swivels, flies, and other lines.

Leader: This monofilament or braided-wire line is used to prevent the shock of a fish's strike from breaking the rest of the line. In panfishing, leaders are sometimes made of lighter material than the main monofilament running line, which prevents loss of all terminal gear when bait fishing brushy areas.

Lunker: A trophy-size game fish.

Lure: Any of an assortment of plugs, spinners, spoons, or jigs, complete with a hook or hooks, used to entice fish into striking.

Plug: A lure, usually made of an elongated piece of wood or plastic, that represents a bait fish.

Reel: A mechanism with a handle to crank in or let out fishing line; it is usually equipped with a gear system or "drag" used to tire a fish.

Release: The act of setting a fish free after it is caught; also, the lever of a fishing reel that allows line to roll free from the spool.

Retrieve: The act of reeling in line.

Rod: A long, pole-like instrument used for casting and playing fish.

Roe: Eggs from a "hen" or spawning female fish, particularly a salmon.

Run: To swim off with the bait.

Setting the hook: The act of lifting a rod upward with the reel's drag engaged to drive the hook into a fish.

Sinker: A fishing weight.

Shank: The long part of a hook.

Slug: A very large sturgeon.

Snag: Usually a branch or log that provides structure for holding game fish, appearing to boaters as an obstacle in the water.

Snap-swivel: A metal clip designed for attaching a line to a lure so that it eliminates line twist caused by the lure's action or by playing a fish.

Spinner: A lure, equipped with a short metal shaft for attaching beads and blades that spin in the water, that is propelled by a river current or a caster reeling it in.

Spool: The cylinder of a fishing reel that stores line.

Spoon: A lure made of shiny metal, sometimes hammered into a design to represent a bait fish, shaped to provide it with action for casting or jigging.

Still fishing: Fishing with bait from the shore or an anchored boat.

Streamer: A large fly pattern, usually made of feathers, synthetic fish hair, or Mylar, designed to represent a bait fish.

Strike: The act of a fish attacking a bait, lure, or fly.

Structure: Geologic formations submerged in lakes, rivers, streams, and bays, holding populations of bait and game fish.

Swivel: A small, metal barrel that connects two wire eyelets and allows line attached to each eyelet to rotate in opposite directions.

Tide: The shifting of water due to the gravitational pull of the sun and moon on the earth's oceans.

Tippet: A tapered monofilament leader to which a fly is attached for fly fishing.

Trolling: The act of dragging lures and sometimes bait behind a moving boat.

Waders: Waterproof boots or stockings, extending above a person's hip or chest, used for wading in streams and rivers; they are often used by fly fishermen who must get adequate back casting distance.

Weight: A sinker or split-shot made of lead and used for presenting lures or bait along the bottoms of rivers and lakes.

Selected references

California Department of Fish and Game. (1981a). *Trout of California*. Sacramento, CA: California Resources Agency.

California Department of Fish and Game. (1981b). *Warmwater game fishes of California*. Sacramento, CA: California Resources Agency.

Henkin, H. (1977). *The complete fisherman's catalog*. Philadelphia: J.B. Lippincott.

International Game Fish Association. (1983). *World record game fishes*. Fort Lauderdale, FL: Author.

Lowrance Electronics, Inc. (1975). *New guide to the fun of electronic fishing*. Tulsa, OK: Author.

McGinnis, S.M. (1984). *Freshwater fishes of California*. Berkeley, CA: University of California Press.

Schwiebert, E. (1984). *Trout tackle two*. New York: E.P. Dutton.

Threinen, C.W. (1960). What kind of fish is that? *Wisconsin Conservation Bulletin*, **25**, 2-10.

Index

About the Author

Keith Rogers has enjoyed recreational fishing since his childhood days in Indiana. That strong interest carried over to his work as a writer for several East San Francisco Bay area newspapers where he wrote weekly fishing columns for six years. Because of his fishing expertise, Keith is often invited to address fishing seminars by local fishing organizations.

Keith studied at Michigan State University where he was a member of the varsity track team. He then served in the U.S. Army before graduating from California State University at Hayward with a degree in mass communications. Keith is presently a staff writer for *The Valley Times*, a newspaper circulated in the Livermore and San Ramon valleys of California. In addition to fishing, he also enjoys snow skiing, wind surfing, backpacking, and running.

About the Author